Level A

Sadlier Vocabulary FOR SUCCESS

Douglas Fisher, Ph.D.

Professor of Language & Literacy Education
School of Teacher Education
San Diego State University
San Diego, CA

Nancy Frey, Ph.D.

Professor of Literacy
School of Teacher Education
San Diego State University
San Diego, CA

PROGRAM CONSULTANTS

Ernest Morrell, Ph.D.

Professor of Education
Urban Schooling Division & I.D.E.A.
Graduate School of Education, University of California
Los Angeles, CA

Rosalie M. Quiñones, M.A. Edu. Lead

ESOL/ELL Consultant
Assistant Principal, Language Arts & Reading
Colonial High School
Orlando, FL

MaryBeth Webeler, Ph.D.

English Language Arts Consultant
Assistant Superintendent for
Curriculum & Instruction
Downers Grove Grade School District 58
Downers Grove, IL

Ann Marie Ginsberg, Ed.D.

Assessment & Technology Consultant
Principal
Turtle Hook Middle School
Uniondale, NY

S® **Sadlier**

Advisers

The publisher wishes to thank the following teachers and administrators, who read portions of the series prior to publication, for their comments and suggestions.

Heather Anderson
English Teacher
San Diego, CA

Sarah Ressler Wright
English Teacher
Delaware, OH

Patricia Stack
English Teacher
South Park, PA

Andrea Canonico
Language Arts Teacher
Hoboken, NJ

Jay Falls
English Teacher
Solon, OH

Siobhan McNulty
Special Education Teacher
New York, NY

Melissa Venezia
Reading Teacher
Canton, GA

Cover Series Design: Silver Editions, Inc.

Photo Credits:
Cover: Dorling Kindersley; Interior: Alamy/David Ball: 114; James Boardman: 232; blickwinkel: 40; Riley Cooney: 190; Danita Delimont: 56 *right*, 56 *left*; Robert W. Ginn: 200 *bottom*; David Grossman: 154; Image-USA: 226; Gunter Marx: 13 *top*; Gail Mooney-Kelly: 37 *left*; Megapress: 13 *bottom*; nagelestock.com: 36 *center*; Eric Nathan: 74, Dave Stamboulis: 118; Stockbyte: 42; H. Mark Weidman Photography: 120; Maximillian Weinzieri: 152 *right*. AP Photo/The Plain Dealer/David I. Andersen: 68. The Art Archive/Museum of London: vi *right*, 124; Private Collection/Gianni Dagli Orti: 210; Ragab Papyrus Institute Cairo/Gianni Dagli Orti: 115 *left*. Art Resource/Alinari: 196 *inset*; Bildarchiv Preussuscher Kulturbesitz: 176 *background*; ©2010 Calder Foundation, New York/Artists Rights Society (ARS), New York: 24; Erich Lessing: 175; Reunion des Musees Nationaux: 177. Courtesy of Denise Schmandt-Besserat, PHD: 176 *inset*. The Bridgeman Art Library/Ashmolean Museum, University of Oxford, UK: 115 *right*; DACS/Index: 36 *right*; Museum of Fine Arts Houston, Texas, USA/Gift of Miss Ima Hogg: 220 *left*; Corbis/Atlantide Phototravel/Guido Cozzi: 209; Bettman: 71; Bettman/Philip Gendreau: 188; Horace Bristol: 56 *center*; Digital Stock Corporation: 12 *background*, 114 *background*, 209 *background*; Encyclopedia: 46; JAI/Walter Bibikow: 211; Randy Faris: 234; Bob Krist: vi *left*, 230–231; Christopher Morris: iv *right*, 125; Jose Fusta Raga: 192; Reuters/Scott Audette: 47 *top*; Reuters/Lana Slivar: 57; Tony Salvino: 221; Science Faction/Ed Darack: 81; Bernd Vogel: 182; Nik Wheeler: 242. Dennis Cox: 104 *top*. Scott Dommin: 80, 81 *background*. DK Images/David Pyne: 116. Dreamstime: 36, 58, 76, 148. The Everett Collection: 197 *right*. The Field Museum, #GN91059_062d/John Weinstein: 162 *top*. Bob Franke: 2–3 *background*. The Granger Collection/Fournier: 34. Getty Images/AFP/Roberto Schmidt: 72; AFP/Chris Wilkins: 91 *boat inset*; Getty Images News/Frederic Dupoux: 70; Flickr/Patrick T. Power Photography: 94; Johner Images: 106; Premium Archive/Ruth Orkin: 16; Stone/Matt Henry Gunther: 176; Stone/Alan Thorton: 82; Taxi/Timelaps/Tony Evans: 152–153; Time & Life Pictures/Evelyn Hofer: 3 *left*, WireImage/Bob Gevinski: 86. The Image Works/Eastcott-Momatiuk: 91; Heritage-Images/Artmedia: iv *left*, 103; NASA/SSPL: iii, 47 *bottom*; VISUM/Alfred Buellesbach: 31 *center*. iStockphoto: 62, 96, 208. Jim Siebold: 37 *right*. Jupiter Images/Brand X Pictures/GK Hart/Vikki Hart: 156. Mary Evans Picture Library/Edwin Mullan Collection: 104 *bottom*. Masterfile: 48, 52. Myrleen Pearson: v *right*, 186–187. NASA/JPL/Space Science Institute: 2, 3 *right*. National Geographic Stock/Peter V. Bianchi: 220 *right*. Photodisc: 152, 153, 175 *background*, 220 *border*. PhotoEdit, Inc./David Young-Wolff: 222. Photographer's Direct/Gerhard Gscheidle Photography: 105. Photolibrary/age fotostock/Javier Larrea: 126; age fotostock/Mike Hill: 69 *bottom*; AlaskaStock: 146; AlaskaStock/Michael DeYoung: 35; De Agostini Editore: 186–187; Glowimages: 28; Imagebriker RF/Christian Heinrich: 212; Index Stock Imagery/Don Stevenson: 128; Index Stock Photography/HMS Group Inc.: 90; Oxford Scientific (OSF)/Sue Scott: 142–143; Juniors Bildarchiv: 8; Peter Arnold Images/Luiz C. Marigo: 174; Peter Arnold Images/David Scharf: 152 *left*; Photography EPC: 130; Sinopictures/Dinodia Dinodia: 136; Superstock: 84; The Travel Library/Mike Kipling: 224; Volvox/Tsuneo Nakamura: 38. Photo Researchers, Inc./Biophoto Associates: 22–23; SPL: 23; Geoff Tompkinson: 60. Photoshot/NHPA: 50. Punchstock/BananaStock: 26; Blend Images: 1, 4, 6, 110, 158, 202; Creatas: 200 *top*; Cultura: 141; Digital Vision: 163; Image Source: 18. Jupiter Images: 180; Photodisc: 216; Photographer's Choice: 102; photosindia: 14, 236; Rubberball: 144; Stockbyte: 103 *background*; Tetra Images: 196. Shutterstock.com: v *left*, 6, 8, 12, 14, 16, 18, 20, 26, 37, 40, 42, 50, 52, 60, 62, 74, 76, 80, 84, 86, 90 *background*, 91 *background*, 92, 94, 96, 100, 104 *background*, 105 *background*, 106, 108, 110, 118, 120, 124 *background*, 130, 142, 143, 144, 146, 148, 153 *right*, 154, 156, 158, 162, 164, 166, 168, 180, 182, 192, 196, 197 *left*, 198, 202, 210 *background*, 211 *background*, 214, 216, 224, 226, 230, 232, 234, 236. Courtesy of Sieman's Foundation/Rebecca Varga Photography: 22. Wikipedia: 230. All page and cover illustration: Shutterstock.com

For additional online resources, go to vocabularyforsuccess.com and enter the Student Access Code VFS11SGVK8TZ

Printed in the United States of America.
ISBN: 978-1-4217-0806-5
123456789 VKS 14 13 12 11 10

Table of Contents

UNIT 1

"Mad" Scientists 1–34

LESSON 1: Scientist of the Cosmos ⟨obituary⟩ 2
approach, assess, bias, construct, distribute, explanation,
haphazard, hypothesis, interpret, issue

LESSON 2: The Global Warming Debate ⟨online editorial⟩ 12
argument, chronology, confer, debate, document, reassess,
reconstruct, redistribute, reinterpret, research

LESSON 3: Teen Earns $40,000 Science Prize ⟨press release⟩ 22
assist, control, cultivate, evident, fulfill, ingenuity,
intern, invaluable, legacy, mobile

ENRICHMENT Synonyms and Antonyms 32
Word Study: Denotation and Connotation 33
Comprehension Check 34

UNIT 2

See the World 35–68

LESSON 4: Travels of the Ancient Romans ⟨travel log⟩ 36
area, barren, feat, fraught, initial, migrate,
prow, stern, vicinity, widespread

LESSON 5: Why Take Risks to Explore? ⟨persuasive essay⟩ 46
claim, embark, entrust, prospect, ransack, transition,
translate, transmit, transport, undertake

LESSON 6: Tsunami! ⟨online feature article⟩ 56
airborne, atlas, enable, global, hemisphere, origin,
retire, restrict, trek, witness

ENRICHMENT Synonyms and Antonyms 66
Word Study: Idioms 67
Comprehension Check 68

UNIT 3 — Natural Disasters 69–102

LESSON 7: Surviving an Earthquake ⟨how-to article⟩ 70
achievable, alter, collide, crust, invariable,
jolt, landscape, mantle, obtainable, signal

LESSON 8: Hurricane Hunters ⟨career profile⟩ 80
aerial, atmosphere, challenge, climate, cycle,
despite, expand, hardship, ordeal, source

LESSON 9: The Great Flood ⟨photo essay⟩ 90
barrier, buoy, debris, deluge, erosion, inaccessible,
incapable, mass, risk, vessel

ENRICHMENT Synonyms and Antonyms 100
Word Study: Proverbs 101
Comprehension Check 102

UNIT 4 — Where Did That Come From? 103–136

LESSON 10: Cai Lun ⟨biography⟩ 104
accurate, compile, contact, correspond, devoted,
encounter, estimate, identical, minimal, portion

LESSON 11: Egyptian Advances in Science ⟨textbook entry⟩ 114
civilization, constellation, counsel, culture, deed, latent,
orient, population, regulation, superlative

LESSON 12: The History of Skates ⟨historical nonfiction⟩ 124
adequate, advance, anticipated, circumstance, compatible,
dominance, foundation, nuisance, plague, trade

ENRICHMENT Synonyms and Antonyms 134
Word Study: Denotation and Connotation 135
Comprehension Check 136

MID-YEAR REVIEW 137–140

UNIT 5

Energy=Life 141–174

LESSON 13: Miraculous Seaweed ⟨expository essay⟩ 142
benefit, ecosystem, energy, factor, likewise, maximum,
minimum, photosynthesis, prone, recreation

LESSON 14: The Dirt Under Your Feet ⟨magazine article⟩ 152
category, consequence, consume, decompose,
fungus, host, impact, infection, parasite, seek

LESSON 15: Conserving Our Resources ⟨letter to the editor⟩ 162
copious, critique, decline, degenerate, deplete,
detect, foster, invade, recycling, species

ENRICHMENT Synonyms and Antonyms 172
Word Study: Idioms 173
Comprehension Check 174

UNIT 6

The Best Ideas From Ancient Times 175–208

LESSON 16: The Write Beginning ⟨nonfiction narrative⟩ 176
bulk, commended, enrich, formal, inferences,
nevertheless, random, report, scribe, uniform

LESSON 17: Citizen for a Day ⟨debate⟩ 186
abnormal, architecture, classic, columns, dignity,
durable, enormous, mosaic, normal, norms

LESSON 18: The Glory That Is Rome ⟨speech⟩ 196
abundant, authority, concept, cornerstone, doctrine,
downfall, impose, plenty, premier, range

ENRICHMENT Synonyms and Antonyms 206
Word Study: Proverbs 207
Comprehension Check 208

UNIT 7

Disappeared! 209–242

LESSON 19: The Mystery of the Minoans ⟨mystery⟩ 210
appalled, appeal, appear, appropriate, credible,
prey, region, reside, theory, variable

LESSON 20: The Anasazi People ⟨encyclopedia entry⟩ 220
ally, apparatus, assault, brink, cease, disperse,
feature, incredible, pare, robust

LESSON 21: The Easter Island Puzzle ⟨interview⟩ 230
bizarre, decode, dramatic, duplicate, implicate,
leisure, motive, premise, reference, ritual

ENRICHMENT Synonyms and Antonyms 240
Word Study: Denotation and Connotation 241
Comprehension Check 242

End-of-Year Review 243–246
Index 247–248

Dear Students:

We're excited about the school year ahead, and we hope you are, too. You've got a new vocabulary book in your hands right now, and we hope you'll take a few minutes to thumb through it as you read this letter. You'll see that *Vocabulary for Success* is different from other vocabulary books you may have seen or used in the past.

The first thing that might catch your eye is the Lesson titles. Each of these topics has been selected to appeal to your interest in the social, physical, and biological worlds around you. The words you will study in *Vocabulary for Success* are related to these topics. The words will help you better understand what you read in school, and out of school, too. They will also help you better express yourself as a writer and as a speaker.

You may also notice that there are quite a few activities in this program that you can do with your classmates. One of the things educators have found is that learning can occur through games and activities.

We're also proud of the video and audio resources that are also available with the program. Learning new words isn't just about someone telling you what they are; you need to experience them in many different ways. Each lesson in *Vocabulary for Success* is accompied by a short video introduction to the words—so you can see and hear them in action. You can also listen to the words being pronounced and used in sentences. Maybe you'll be inspired to make your own vocabulary videos and podcasts!

One last thing: we organized the word lists so that you can learn words independently, too. No vocabulary program could teach you all the words you'll need to know, and that's really not how people learn most vocabulary, anyway. This program is designed to help you become a better independent word learner. People learn new vocabulary in a variety of ways. At times, figuring out an unknown word by figuring out the parts you do know is a great strategy. At other times, the clues around the unknown word can tip you off to the meaning. And don't forget resources like dictionaries.

Whether you aspire to be an engineer, scientist, artist, musician, educator, or athlete, your ability to express your ideas is the key to your success. That's where the title came from—*Vocabulary for Success*.

Douglas Fisher and Nancy Frey

Pronunciation Key

The pronunciation is indicated for every basic word introduced in this book. Single letters or combinations of letters, as listed below, are used to represent sounds and are similar to those appearing in many dictionaries that use student-friendly pronunciations.

Of course, there are many English words for which two or more pronunciations are commonly accepted. For all such words in this book, the authors have sought to make things easier for students by giving just one pronunciation. The only significant exception occurs when the pronunciation changes with a shift in the part of speech. Thus we would show that *appropriate* in the adjective form is pronounced *uh-PROH-pree-uht*, and the noun form, *uh-PROH-pree-ayt*. Note that the major stressed syllable is represented by capital letters.

Vowels							
	a	hat	ee	feet, beat	oo	room, rule, pull
	ah	father	i	sit	or	torn, pore
	air	hair, dare, chance	ihr	gear, mere	oy	boy, soil
			eye	island, tile, bye, pie, fly	ou	pouch, cow
	ar	park			u	put, look
	ay	say, main, fade, cape	o	pot	uh	cut, about, lotion
			oh	doe, though, bone, roam	ur	urge, heard, corner
	aw	saw, fraught, cough			yoo	cue, you, muse, fuel
	e	ten				

Consonants							
	b	bore, crib	m	mine, ram	t	tin, fit
	ch	chore, hitch, which	n	not, thin, knife, gnome	th	thick, faith
	d	deal, had	ng	thing	th	than, rather, clothe
	f	feed, off, enough	p	pit, trap	v	vine, rave, of
	g	give, rag	r	race, star	w	wise, wharf
	h	her	s	sing, face, cellar	y	yam
	j	jelly, bridge, giant	ss	mass, face, gas	z	zoo, is, choose
	k	kid, trick, card	sh	shape, fish	zh	pleasure
	l	line, fill				

Stress   The syllable receiving the major stress is capitalized:
FOH-kuhss, kon-sti-TOO-shuhn

Abbreviations   *adj.* adjective   *adv.* adverb   *n.* noun   *v.* verb

Online Components

vocabularyforsuccess.com

Note: A spoken pronunciation of each key is also available by going to **vocabularyforsuccess.com**. The **Online Audio and Video Program** permits you to hear not only the pronunciation of each word, but also its definition and an example of its usage in a sentence. You also can watch a video introduction of each word. With iWords you can listen to one word at a time or download all of the words of a Unit, and listen to the audio program at your convenience.

"Mad" Scientists

LESSON 1

Scientist of the Cosmos

Carl Sagan changed the way we look at life—in outer space.

approach	distribute	hypothesis
assess	explanation	interpret
bias	haphazard	issue
construct		

LESSON 2

The Global Warming Debate

Governments are working together to help save the planet.

argument	document	redistribute
chronology	reassess	reinterpret
confer	reconstruct	research
debate		

LESSON 3

Teen Earns $40,000 Science Prize

A high school student's research may one day help treat cancer.

assist	fulfill	invaluable
control	ingenuity	legacy
cultivate	intern	mobile
evident		

▶ **Watch** a video introduction to this passage at **vocabularyforsuccess.com**.

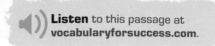 **Listen** to this passage at **vocabularyforsuccess.com**.

Scientist of the Cosmos

<obituary>

A giant in the field of space science is dead. On December 20th, 1996, Carl Sagan, age 62, died after a two-year illness. From the time he was a small boy, Sagan was intrigued by the concept of life on other planets. The issue of whether there is intelligent life in the universe was compelling to him. In order to prepare for his career, Sagan studied biology, physics, astronomy, and astrophysics in college.

Sagan was among the first scientists to make the following hypothesis: There might be oceans of liquid compounds on one of Saturn's moons. Sagan thought that if this proved to be true, this moon might be habitable. Additionally, Sagan began to construct theories about the danger of global warming. His ideas were based on the discovery of very hot greenhouse gases on Venus. As Sagan began to assess the situation—that this was part of the natural development of Venus—he began to fear that Earth might develop the same way.

Sagan was not just a scientist. He was also a TV star. Sagan is probably best known for his popular television series, *Cosmos*. His goal was to help people understand the universe. His ability to give a clear explanation about outer space made the series very popular. He helped interpret difficult ideas about the cosmos and made them easy for people to understand. Sagan's approach made science exciting

VOCABULARY

issue	interpret
hypothesis	approach
construct	distribute
assess	bias
explanation	haphazard

and enjoyable. He thought that if he could distribute his scientific work, more people would become interested in pursuing and studying the subject.

Sagan believed that the stakes were very high as to whether or not there was extraterrestrial life. That is why his bias was to demand that scientists use thorough standards of evidence. There could be nothing haphazard or careless about the research. Carl Sagan was a great researcher and a wonderful teacher to us all. He will be greatly missed.

TALK ABOUT IT

With a partner, answer the questions below. Use as many of the highlighted words in the selection as you can.

1. What do you think of Sagan's *approach* to teaching people about science?

2. What *issue* would you like to be remembered for?

Astronomer Carl Sagan changed the way that people viewed space.

vocabularyforsuccess.com

▶ **Watch** a video introduction for each word

◀)) **Listen** to iWords

📖 **Refer** to the online dictionary

Word Meanings

For each highlighted word on pages 2–3, the meaning is given below. For practice with other meanings, see pages 7–9. For synonyms and antonyms, see page 32.

1. issue
(ISH-oo)

(n.) An *issue* is a subject or matter of concern about which people often disagree.

(v.) When you *issue* something, you send it out, give it out, or publish it.

2. hypothesis
(hye-POTH-uh-siss)

(n.) A *hypothesis* is a statement or prediction that can be tested and studied.

3. construct
v. (kuhn-STRUHKT)
n. (KON-struhkt)

(v.) When you *construct* something, you make it, build it, or put it together.

(n.) A *construct* is something carefully put together, such as an important idea.

4. assess
(uh-SESS)

(v.) If you *assess* something, you look at it closely to judge its value, quality, or importance.

5. explanation
(ek-spluh-NAY-shuhn)

(n.) An *explanation* is a statement that makes things clear or easier to understand.

6. interpret
(in-TUR-prit)

(v.) When you *interpret* something, you figure out what it means, and you may share its meaning with others.

7. approach
(uh-PROHCH)

(n.) Your *approach* is your way of doing something.

(v.) When you *approach* something, you move nearer to it or closer in time.

8. distribute
(diss-TRIB-yoot)

(v.) When you *distribute* something, you give it to others or spread it around.

9. bias
(BYE-uhs)

(n.) If you prefer one thing above another and make judgments based on your own preferences, you have a *bias*.

(v.) To *bias* a person means to give him a slanted way of thinking because of favoring one person or point of view more than another. Similarly, a *bias* line on a piece of cloth is slanted or diagonal.

10. haphazard
(hap-HAZ-urd)

(adj.) Something that is done in a *haphazard* way is not planned and lacks order or direction.

Word Talk

Each lesson word has been placed in a category. With a partner, discuss and list items that belong in each category. Compare your results with those of another pair of students.

Issues That Affect Students	Interesting Scientific *Hypotheses*

Items You Can *Construct*	Objects You Can *Assess*	Events That Might Need an *Explanation*	Things That Need to Be *Interpreted*

Good *Approaches* to Studying	Ways to *Distribute* Classroom Information	Selections Made Based on a *Bias*	Occurrences That Seem *Haphazard*

Check for Understanding

Choose the lesson word that completes each sentence. Write the word on the line provided. Some words will be used twice.

approach	construct	hypothesis
assess	distribute	interpret
bias	explanation	issue
	haphazard	

1. I get confused and disorganized if I do homework in a/an _____ way.

2. My friend's _____ to sports is to try a few different ones, but I like to focus on basketball.

3. I looked up many words in the dictionary in order to _____ the text.

4. The editor's slanted opinion shows a/an _____ against the mayor.

5. The recipe gives a/an _____ that clearly describes each step in making the cake.

6. We were told to think of a scientific _____ and test it.

7. My aunt helped me _____ the Spanish poem so I could understand it.

8. People in the neighborhood argued for months about the _____ of widening the streets.

9. The students will _____ the quality of their stories by reading them aloud and asking for comments.

10. The company will _____ free samples to each home.

11. I'll edit my draft and _____ a plot with more action.

12. We all agree about the need for a new car, so it isn't a/an _____ for us.

Expand Word Meanings

Read the paragraph below to learn other meanings for some of the lesson words.

When scientists work together to come up with a construct that shapes the world, we might not understand their thinking—but we feel the effects. Scientific thinking has changed our lives. It has produced amazing inventions and life-saving medicines. Because of science, we can watch a space vehicle approach a faraway planet or view stars in deep space. I don't want to bias others into agreeing with me, but I consider scientists to be heroes. America should issue a letter of thanks to its scientists. Without them, our world would be a very different place!

Some words from the lesson are used in a different way here. For example, *construct* is used as a noun that means "something carefully put together, such as an important idea." Can you figure out the meaning of the other highlighted words as they are used here? Refer to page 4 to confirm meanings.

Apply Other Meanings

Complete each sentence with a highlighted word from the paragraph above.

1. I don't want to _____ you, but you may agree that my brother is the best swimmer on the team.

2. The United States government is a/an _____ of the Founding Fathers that we still use today.

3. When you _____ our house from the street, the driveway looks very steep.

4. The newspaper will _____ a special edition to cover the election results.

5. Some cat owners try to _____ people into agreeing that cats are smarter than dogs.

6. As visitors _____ the art museum, they often stop to look at the colorful flower beds.

7. The principal will _____ an announcement if school closes due to severe weather.

8. Mother doesn't want to _____ me, but she would like me to pick the less expensive shoes.

9. The character was a literary _____ that made the book more believable.

10. If you _____ the horse slowly, you may be able to stroke its neck.

Word Associations

Use what you know about the lesson word in italics to answer each question. Circle the letter next to the phrase that best answers the question. Be prepared to explain your answers.

1. Which assignment may include a *hypothesis* for further study?

   a. written narrative

   b. set of math problems

   c. science experiment

2. Which action often takes place in a *haphazard* way?

   a. tossing out garbage

   b. exercising

   c. school testing

3. Which is likely to be an *issue* for a small restaurant?

   a. fresh ingredients

   b. seating space

   c. friendly servers

4. Which item does a person have a company *distribute* to his or her home?

   a. newspaper

   b. automobile fuel

   c. clothing

5. Which situation would require an *explanation*?

   a. getting a good grade

   b. scoring a point in a game

   c. arriving late for school

6. Which item would you study carefully in order to *assess* its value?

   a. dollar bill

   b. soccer ball

   c. used car

7. Which item do people *construct*?

   a. tree

   b. skyscraper

   c. riverbank

8. What might be difficult to *interpret* in a foreign country?

   a. artwork

   b. a cell phone ring tone

   c. a restaurant menu

9. Which wild animal is easiest to *approach*?

   a. turtle

   b. bird

   c. deer

10. Which group may have a strong *bias* about a new school library?

    a. bus drivers

    b. teachers

    c. sports team

8

Check Again

Use what you know about the lesson word in italics to complete each sentence. Be sure your sentences make sense.

1. I know there is *bias* in the article I'm reading when _____

_____

2. My *approach* to doing homework is _____

3. A driver who steers in a *haphazard* way is likely to _____

4. One way I can make a *hypothesis* is _____

5. A grocery shopper might *assess* fruit by _____

6. A good *explanation* of how crystals form might be found _____

_____

7. The first thing I do when my teachers *distribute* a test is _____

_____

8. Good writers *construct* a well-written paragraph by _____

_____

9. An *issue* that teenagers and parents might not agree on is _____

_____

10. Something I might not be able to *interpret* in a foreign country is _____

Challenge Yourself

Follow the directions to write sentences with the lesson words in italics. Be sure your sentences make sense both grammatically and in meaning.

1. Write a sentence using the word *hypothesis*.

2. Write a sentence that is exactly eight words in length using the word *distribute*.

3. Write an eight-word sentence using the word *haphazard* in the seventh position.

Word-Solving Strategies:
Context Clues

Punctuation

Sometimes you can use punctuation marks to help you find clues about unfamiliar words in a reading selection.

> Sagan was among the first scientists to make this hypothesis: There might be oceans of liquid compounds on the moon of Saturn.

Notice the colon after **hypothesis**. The colon lets you know that an example of a hypothesis will follow. You can use the example to figure out what **a hypothesis is**. Other marks that signal context clues are quotation marks, commas, dashes, and parentheses.

Commas after a word can often be clues to a definition, but commas do not always indicate that a word is being defined.

Claire put on her helmet, hopped on her bike, and pedaled down the street.

"Hopped on her bike" does not define *helmet*. It is part of a series of events.

BE CAREFUL!

Practice

A. Write a highlighted word or phrase and punctuation clue in the first two columns. Using the context clues, write the meaning of the word in the third column.

> Saturn is one of the most recognized planets in the solar system. It is named for the Roman god of agriculture (crop production). Saturn's rings are composed, or made up of, ice and rocky ice-covered bits. Saturn belongs to a group of planets called "Jovian planets." This group of giant planets also includes Jupiter, Uranus, and Neptune. Unlike our own terrestrial planet of Earth, Jovian planets do not have land.

WORD/PHRASE	PUNCTUATION	MEANING

B. Write a sentence for each of the highlighted words from the paragraph above. Use punctuation marks to signal the context clues.

1. _____

2. _____

3. _____

4. _____

Practice for Tests

Fill in the bubble next to the answer that best completes the sentence or answers the question.

1. Read this sentence.

   Our assignment was to *construct* an atomic model for science class.

   Construct means:
   - **A** invent
   - **B** build
   - **C** discuss
   - **D** take apart

2. To *distribute* something, you must:
   - **A** give it out
   - **B** gather it together
   - **C** print it out
   - **D** shorten it

3. The opposite of *haphazard* is:
   - **A** jumbled
   - **B** organized
   - **C** accidental
   - **D** frequent

4. In order to *interpret* something correctly, you must:
   - **A** enjoy it
   - **B** be curious about it
   - **C** value it
   - **D** understand it

5. A term associated with *hypothesis* is:
   - **A** a certainty
   - **B** an angle
   - **C** an estimate
   - **D** a fact

6. Read this sentence.

   Our *approach* for solving the problem was to take a vote.

   In this sentence, *approach* means:
   - **A** way of doing things
   - **B** move nearer to
   - **C** get closer in time
   - **D** only choice

7. An *explanation* does NOT:
   - **A** make things clearer
   - **B** complicate a subject
   - **C** support understanding
   - **D** restate ideas in plain language

8. A topic becomes an *issue* when people:
   - **A** laugh about it
   - **B** forget it
   - **C** read about it
   - **D** disagree about it

9. An investigator with a *bias* would NOT:
   - **A** make quick judgments
   - **B** ignore details
   - **C** check facts
   - **D** overlook evidence

10. One reason to *assess* an object is to:
    - **A** learn its value
    - **B** determine who owns it
    - **C** share it with others
    - **D** prevent it from being stolen

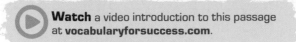
Watch a video introduction to this passage at **vocabularyforsuccess.com**.

Listen to this passage at **vocabularyforsuccess.com**.

The Global Warming Debate
<online editorial>

Nearly everyone has heard of global warming. Many well-known scientists have studied this topic and shared their knowledge. Their research has shown that Earth's temperature is rising. This increase in temperature is producing many harmful effects. These include the rise in serious tornadoes, hurricanes, and other weather disasters around the world.

The issue of global warming is not a new one. In fact, scientists have been studying global warming for many years. However, there is a growing debate about what steps should be taken. There is also a lot of argument about how quickly countries should take action. As the chronology, or sequence of events, unfolds many scientists think that the world must act as quickly as possible. Scientists and politicians have held talks with leaders around the world. They have tried to persuade heads of governments to do something.

In December 2009, more than 120 world leaders held a summit, or meeting, to confer about what should be done. They wanted to reassess the issues and negotiate solutions. World leaders tried to reach a decision about the best ways to address the problems. What happened in Copenhagen has changed the way countries around the world are viewing the challenges. Politicians used to say, "We'll take action if you take action." Now, more are saying, "We all must act together."

The document that came out of the December 2009 conference is called the Copenhagen Accord. It calls for nations around the world to redistribute their efforts in order to stop global warming. Most important is that countries around the world will try to reinterpret how they make and use energy.

New ways to make energy will be studied. Builders will reconstruct older cities, towns, and roads with new "green" ways of building. Scientists think that if everyone around the world helps a little, our efforts will add up to a big change.

Many people believe that conserving energy and creating new sources of energy can slow down global warming.

VOCABULARY

research
debate
argument
chronology
confer

reassess
document
redistribute
reinterpret
reconstruct

TALK ABOUT IT

With a partner, answer the questions below. Use as many of the highlighted words in the selection as you can.

1. If you were to have a *debate* on global warming, what would you say?

2. How has global warming caused you to *reassess* your ideas about the weather?

LESSON 2

Word Meanings

vocabularyforsuccess.com
▶ **Watch** a video introduction for each word
◀)) **Listen** to iWords
▌ **Refer** to the online dictionary

For each highlighted word on pages 12–13, the meaning is given below.
For practice with other meanings, see pages 17–19. For synonyms and
antonyms, see page 32.

1. research
(REE-surch)

(n.) *Research* is a careful search or a close study for information.

(v.) When you *research* a subject, you study it closely or search for information about it.

2. debate
(di-BAYT)

(n.) A *debate* is a discussion in which people take different sides.

(v.) When you *debate*, you talk to others about an issue and voice your opinion.

3. argument
(AR-gyoo-ment)

(n.) When people have an *argument*, they disagree and sometimes get angry.

(n.) An *argument* can also be a reason or explanation for or against something.

4. chronology
(kruh-NOL-ah-jee)

(n.) In a *chronology*, events are arranged in time order.

5. confer
(kuhn-FUR)

(v.) When you *confer* with others, you meet with them to share ideas or ask for advice.

6. reassess
(ree-uh-SESS)

(v.) When you *reassess* something, you look back to review it, especially if it has changed or you have new information.

7. document
n. (DOK-yuh-muhnt)
v. (DOK-yuh-ment)

(n.) A *document* gives information or proof in written form. A computer file might also be called a *document*.

(v.) When you *document* something, you record information about it or provide evidence for it.

8. redistribute
(ree-diss-TRIB-yoot)

(v.) When you give something out again or spread it around in a different way, you *redistribute* it.

9. reinterpret
(ree-in-TUR-prit)

(v.) If you *reinterpret* something, you find a new or different meaning for it.

10. reconstruct
(ree-kuhn-STRUHKT)

(v.) When you *reconstruct* something, you make, build, or put it together again.

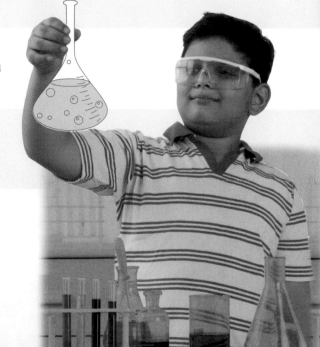

Each lesson word is listed here. With a partner, take turns drawing a picture to illustrate the meaning of six of the words. As one partner draws, the other partner identifies the vocabulary word.

argument

chronology

confer

debate (n.)

document (n.)

reassess

reconstruct

redistribute

reinterpret

research (n.)

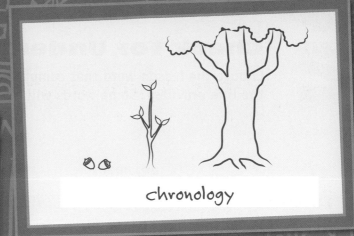

chronology

Check for Understanding

Choose the lesson word that completes each sentence. Write the word on the line provided. Some words will be used twice.

argument	debate	redistribute
chronology	document	reinterpret
confer	reassess	research
	reconstruct	

E=MC²

1. The _____ of Einstein's life begins with his birth in Germany.

2. If we _____ the work so each of us does some of it, Juan won't have to work over the weekend to finish the project.

3. My birth certificate is an important _____ that tells where I was born.

4. I used approved Web sites for my _____ on Albert Einstein.

5. In the _____ between the candidates for Student Council President, I support the person who wants to hold more dances after school.

6. I met with my science teacher to _____ about how to improve my final grade.

7. The city will use steel and concrete to _____ the old wooden bridge.

8. To recognize the importance of exercise, I had to _____ its benefits.

9. The neighbors' _____ began with a disagreement over fences.

10. Dad reviewed the _____ of the car trouble and found it began on our last vacation.

11. I thought I understood the essay, but a second reading helped me _____ the meaning.

12. If we _____ the playground, we can make it safer for young children.

Expand Word Meanings

Read the paragraph below to learn other meanings for some of the lesson words.

At one time people believed that Earth was at the center of the universe. Then in the 1500s, Copernicus presented the argument that planets travel around the sun. Copernicus would document his ideas in a book published at the end of his life. Galileo spoke out for Copernicus's ideas in the 1600s, but other people would debate the ideas and call them false or dangerous. Galileo decided to research astronomy and knew Copernicus was right. His continued support for Copernicus's ideas forced him into house arrest, where he spent the last years of his life.

! Some words from the lesson are used in a different way here. For example, in this paragraph the noun *argument* means "a reason or explanation for or against something." Can you figure out the meaning of the other highlighted words as they are used here? Refer to page 14 to confirm meanings.

Apply Other Meanings

Complete each sentence with a highlighted word from the paragraph above.

1. I supported my _____ for recycling with facts, figures, and examples from my own neighborhood.

2. The traveler will _____ his trip with journal entries and postcards to friends.

3. I used an encyclopedia and magazine articles to _____ information about Saudi Arabia.

4. The students will have the chance to share their ideas when they _____ the dress code with the principal.

5. I went to the library to _____ my topic and found lots of information that I could use for my report.

6. News crews from around the state came to town to _____ the opening of the new airport.

7. Citizens who have read the facts support the mayor's _____ for new city buses.

8. My parents say that they will not _____ the curfew issue, so I must be home by 9:00 p.m.

9. Scientists have spent hours in the lab in order to _____ ways to treat illnesses.

10. A reporter followed the President so she could _____ the leader's workday.

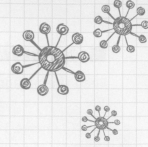

Word Associations

Use what you know about the lesson word in italics to answer each question. Circle the letter next to the phrase that best answers the question. Be prepared to explain your answers.

1. Which describes how people sometimes feel during an *argument*?

   a. annoyed
   b. disappointed
   c. hopeful

2. Where is the best place to do *research* on scientist Marie Curie?

   a. bookstore
   b. science lab
   c. library

3. What is the order of items in a *chronology*?

   a. size order
   b. order of importance
   c. time order

4. Which item can someone *reconstruct?*

   a. shattered mirror
   b. car engine
   c. ancient wall painting

5. Which event would TV news programs be most likely to *document*?

   a. town meeting
   b. pep rally
   c. presidential speech

6. How might the school *redistribute* money after a fundraiser?

   a. keep it
   b. give it to the person who buys equipment
   c. have a meeting about what to do

7. Which might you *reinterpret* after giving some thought to it?

   a. shopping list
   b. table of contents
   c. poem

8. Which might be a subject for *debate* between parents and teenagers?

   a. use of the Internet
   b. math problems
   c. soccer rules

9. What common situation might make you *reassess* your plans to go camping?

   a. the Ice Age
   b. change in seasons
   c. rainy weather

10. What is a student most likely to *confer* with a teacher about?

    a. sports
    b. an assignment
    c. the lunchroom menu

Check Again

Use what you know about the lesson word in italics to complete each sentence. Be sure your sentences make sense.

1. If I need to *reinterpret* a scene from Shakespeare, I might _____

_____

2. When coaches and players *confer*, they often _____

3. Scientists who *research* weather _____

_____

4. Some people *document* their life by _____

5. If I were going to *reconstruct* our school, I would _____

_____

6. The *chronology* of a president might include _____

7. An *argument* between friends might end when _____

8. After getting a poor grade, a student might *reassess* _____

_____

9. I can *redistribute* things I don't need by _____

10. In order to *debate* an issue, a person should _____

_____

Challenge Yourself

Write Your Own

Follow the directions to write sentences with the lesson words in italics. Be sure your sentences make sense both grammatically and in meaning.

1. Write a sentence using the word *chronology*.

2. Write a sentence that is exactly twelve words in length using the word *reassess*.

3. Write a ten-word sentence using the word *research* in the sixth position.

Word-Solving Strategies:
Prefixes

The prefix re-: "again, anew," "back, backward"

A prefix is a word part that is added to the beginning of a word. Each prefix has its own meaning or meanings. For example, the prefix *re-* can mean "again, anew" or "back, backward." When a prefix is added to the beginning of a word, it changes the meaning of that word.

Let's look at the word *reconstruct* from this lesson. The verb *construct* means "to make, build, or put together." When the prefix *re-* is added to the beginning of *construct*, a new word is formed—*reconstruct*. The new word includes the meaning of the prefix. When you *reconstruct* something, you make, build, or put it together again.

Now let's examine the word *reinterpret* from this lesson. When you *interpret* something, you figure out what it means.

Adding the prefix *re-* to *interpret* changes the meaning of the word. You know that *re-* can mean "again, anew." What does the word *reinterpret* mean? When you reinterpret something, you interpret it again or anew.

Examples

Think about how adding the prefix *re-* changes the meaning of each word from Lesson 1 below.

assess → reassess
distribute → redistribute
issue → reissue

Now look at these words.

view → review
new → renew
acquaint → reacquaint

In some words, combining the meanings of the prefix and the base word won't give you the word's meaning. One example is the verb *research*, which means "to search for information about a subject," not "to search again." It comes from an old French word meaning "to go about seeking." Use context clues if you are unsure of word meaning.

BE CAREFUL!

Practice

Use what you've learned about the prefix *re-* and your knowledge of base words to write the meaning of the following words.

1. rewrite _____

2. return _____

3. rebound _____

4. repay _____

5. regroup _____

6. reconsider _____

7. recall _____

8. reemploy _____

9. retrace _____

10. regain _____

Practice for Tests

Fill in the bubble next to the answer that best completes the sentence or answers the question.

1. Read this sentence.

   When the leaders *confer,* they will talk about the cost of health care.

   Confer means:
   - ○ **A** speak on the phone
   - ○ **B** travel together
   - ○ **C** meet for discussion
   - ○ **D** take a break from work

2. In which activity does one *redistribute* items?
   - ○ **A** a phone conversation
   - ○ **B** a card game
   - ○ **C** a gymnastics competition
   - ○ **D** a hike

3. A group of facts is a *chronology* if:
   - ○ **A** the facts are funny
   - ○ **B** the facts are hard to believe
   - ○ **C** the facts are difficult to research
   - ○ **D** the facts are in time order

4. A word closely associated with *argument* is:
   - ○ **A** disagreement
   - ○ **B** patience
   - ○ **C** cooperation
   - ○ **D** disappointment

5. Which is NOT a *document*?
   - ○ **A** passport
   - ○ **B** birth certificate
   - ○ **C** newspaper
   - ○ **D** movie

6. Read this sentence.

   Scientists and the fishing industry *debate* the problem of overfishing.

   Debate means:
   - ○ **A** discuss sides of an issue
   - ○ **B** agree upon
   - ○ **C** fight about bitterly
   - ○ **D** present ideas in writing

7. You might *reassess* your goals if:
   - ○ **A** you are certain of your future
   - ○ **B** your life remains the same
   - ○ **C** your life changes
   - ○ **D** you haven't made a plan

8. An unreliable resource for *research* is:
   - ○ **A** an encyclopedia volume
   - ○ **B** a blog
   - ○ **C** a government Web site
   - ○ **D** a scientific study

9. Something that one can't *reconstruct* is:
   - ○ **A** a kitchen cabinet
   - ○ **B** a highway exit ramp
   - ○ **C** an airport terminal
   - ○ **D** a forest of mature trees

10. If you *reinterpret* the rules of a game, you might:
   - ○ **A** ask others about the rules
   - ○ **B** play as you have always played
   - ○ **C** play in a different way
   - ○ **D** ignore the rules

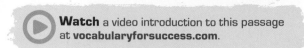
Watch a video introduction to this passage at **vocabularyforsuccess.com**.

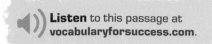
Listen to this passage at **vocabularyforsuccess.com**.

Teen Earns $40,000 Science Prize

‹press release›

For immediate release: Marissa Suchyta, a 17-year-old high school student from Illinois, won third place at a major competition in math, science, and technology. This contest has a long legacy of rewarding outstanding talent in young people from around the country.

Among the many student projects on display describing scientific research, Suchyta's science project stood out. She studied the role of a protein in the human body. This protein is called Geminin. It prevents cells from dividing. Her invaluable research may one day assist researchers seeking new treatments for diseases like cancer. After Suchyta learned that her ingenuity helped her to win her a $40,000 scholarship, she said that this money would help her pay for college.

The chairman of the competition spoke about everyone who took part. He said that it is evident, or plain to see, that the competitors' "dedication to excellence and passion for math and science will no doubt change the world." Suchyta said that she would fulfill her dream if she can continue working in the field of cancer research. She also said that it was "a great experience to be able to share my research with such a large scientific community." Suchyta was encouraged to find herself around so many other students who enjoy science as much as she does.

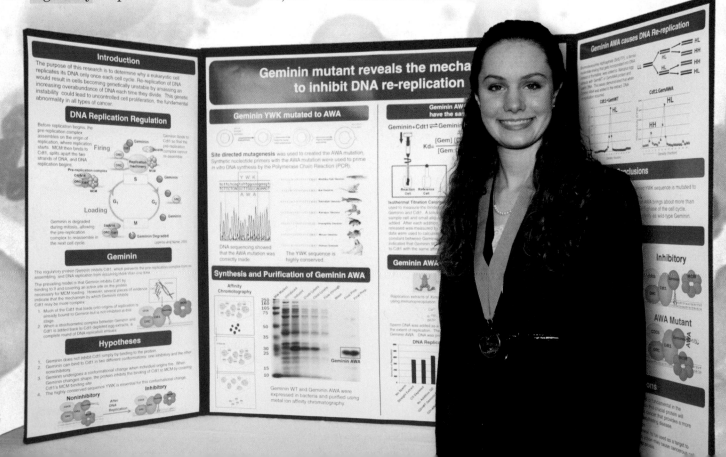

VOCABULARY

legacy	fulfill
invaluable	mobile
assist	intern
ingenuity	cultivate
evident	control

Suchyta has been interested in science for many years. She started the Midwest chapter of the American Cancer Society's "High Schools Against Cancer" campaign. She also founded a group that donates gift baskets to teenagers with cancer. These young people are not mobile when they are in the hospital for treatment, so such gifts are much appreciated.

Suchyta hopes to intern in a hospital and then go on to study medicine. One day she would like to become a brain surgeon as well as get a Ph.D. in science. There's no doubt that her prize money will help cultivate that dream. Clearly, Suchyta has control of her future!

TALK ABOUT IT

With a partner, answer the questions below. Use as many of the highlighted words in the selection as you can.

1. How will the prize money help Marissa *fulfill* her dream to study medicine?

2. In what ways do you think Marissa's *ingenuity* will help her in the future?

Cancer cells dividing. Left: Marissa Suchyta stands in front of her prize-winning science research project.

vocabularyforsuccess.com
▶ **Watch** a video introduction for each word
🔊 **Listen** to iWords 🎧
📖 **Refer** to the online dictionary

Word Meanings

For each highlighted word on pages 22–23, the meaning is given below. For practice with other meanings, see pages 27–29. For synonyms and antonyms, see page 32.

1. legacy
(LEG-uh-see)

(n.) A *legacy* is something handed down from the past. A *legacy* can also be something left to you in a will.

2. invaluable
(in-VAL-yuh-buhl)

(adj.) Something *invaluable* is priceless. Its worth can't be measured.

3. assist
(uh-SIST)

(v.) When you *assist* in something, you help get it done.

4. ingenuity
(in-ji-NOO-i-tee)

(n.) A person who has *ingenuity* is skillful, clever, and good at solving problems.

5. evident
(EV-uh-dent)

(adj.) If something is *evident*, it is clear or plain to see.

6. fulfill
(fuhl-FIL)

(v.) When you *fulfill* something like a goal or a dream, you meet it or make it happen. When you *fulfill* a duty, you do what needs to be done.

7. mobile
adj. (MOH-buhl)
n. (MOH-beeul)

(adj.) If someone or something is *mobile*, that person or thing can move or be moved.

(n.) A *mobile* is a sculpture or object that is constructed with parts that hang and move in the air.

8. intern
(IN-turn)

(v.) When you *intern* at a job, you get on-the-job training while working with experts.

(n.) A person who learns by working on a job is called an *intern*. A new doctor working in a hospital is often called an *intern*.

9. cultivate
(KUHL-tuh-vate)

(v.) When you *cultivate* something, you nurture it and help it. You can *cultivate* a dream, a friendship, or an appreciation or understanding of a topic.

(v.) When you *cultivate* land, you grow crops on it or get it ready for planting. When you *cultivate* plants, you grow them.

10. control
(kuhn-TROHL)

(n.) *Control* is management, guidance, or power over something.

(v.) When you *control* something, you have power over it or can hold it back.

Word Talk

Each lesson word has been placed in a category. With a partner, discuss and list items that belong in each category. Compare your results with those of another pair of students.

Things That Give You *Control*	Ways to *Assist* in Class

Legacies Handed Down to Americans	People with *Ingenuity*	Qualities *Evident* in Leaders	Athletic Dreams to *Fulfill*

Places to *Intern*	*Invaluable* Items for Students	Things That Make You *Mobile*	Ways to *Cultivate* Friendship

Check for Understanding

Choose the lesson word that completes each sentence. Write the word on the line provided. Some words will be used twice.

assist	evident	invaluable
control	fulfill	legacy
cultivate	ingenuity	mobile
	intern	

1. The food bank has a/an _____ of giving that began many years ago.

2. We can't repay the _____ help of all our friends who worked with us.

3. Volunteering at the art museum helped me _____ a love for sculpture.

4. It became _____ that the child was tired when he began to yawn.

5. The café will be open late to _____ the needs of hungry concert-goers.

6. Scrub nurses _____ in the operating room, handing doctors the instruments they need during surgery.

7. _____ of takeoffs and landings comes from the tower near the runway.

8. After medical school, my brother will _____ at a hospital in Chicago.

9. Patients with broken legs become _____ once they learn to use crutches.

10. The long line at the box office made it _____ that the movie was a success.

11. The team's _____ of victory ended this year.

12. It takes _____ to make a doghouse from leftover wood scraps.

Expand Word Meanings

Read the paragraph below to learn other meanings for some of the lesson words.

Can you cultivate a patch of land and turn it into a beautiful flower garden? Do you know how to control weeds without using harmful chemicals? Can you create a hanging garden mobile that will help scare away birds that nibble on our strawberry plants? Are you ready to get your hands dirty, have fun, and boost your knowledge of plants? If so, don't delay. Join us this summer as an intern at the University Research Gardens. All students enrolled in science courses at the university are welcome! Stop in and pick up an application today.

> **!** Some of the words in this lesson are used here in a different way. For example, in this paragraph the verb *cultivate* means "prepare land and grow plants on it." Can you figure out the meaning of the other highlighted words as they are used here? Refer to page 24 to confirm meanings.

Apply Other Meanings

Complete each sentence with a highlighted word from the paragraph above.

1. The dangling _____ twirled in the air whenever a museum visitor walked past it.

2. The farmer used a tractor to _____ his fields for the first spring crops.

3. You can stay healthy and _____ the spread of cold and flu germs by washing your hands often.

4. The _____ joined more experienced doctors in assessing the patient's troubling condition.

5. This year my aunt hopes to _____ prize-winning roses and other flowers in large, sunny gardens.

6. The job as a/an _____ pays little but gives me the chance to learn from the best scientists in the field.

7. The _____ created by American artist Alexander Calder has metal shapes hung from wires and rods.

8. Volunteers used sandbags to hold back the floodwater and _____ its flow.

9. If you do not _____ the land, wildflowers and weeds may grow on it.

10. My little brother made a hanging _____ using paper, string, and a coat hanger.

Word Associations

Use what you know about the lesson word in italics to answer each question. Circle the letter next to the phrase that best answers the question. Be prepared to explain your answers.

1. Which activity does NOT take *ingenuity* ?
   a. creating a new recipe
   b. fixing a flat tire
   c. designing a Web site

2. Which person might take a job as an *intern* in an office?
   a. teacher
   b. college student
   c. senior citizen

3. Which makes it *evident* that a storm is on the way?
   a. large dark clouds
   b. low temperature
   c. mist or fog

4. Which work is always *mobile*?
   a. road repair
   b. toll booth clerk
   c. pizza delivery

5. Which might be part of the *legacy* of a will?
   a. antique piano
   b. musical talent
   c. a grandfather's sense of humor

6. Which can *fulfill* your need for vitamins?
   a. exercise
   b. water
   c. food

7. Which is *invaluable* to the success of a sports team?
   a. practice time
   b. new uniforms
   c. cheering crowd

8. Which might you *cultivate* in a backyard garden?
   a. wheat
   b. tomatoes
   c. grass

9. Which can a player *control* while bowling?
   a. alley
   b. pins
   c. ball

10. What might you do if you *assist* a librarian?
   a. bring books back on time
   b. shelve books
   c. write research reports

Check Again

Use what you know about the lesson word in italics to complete each sentence. Be sure your sentences make sense.

1. Library texts are *invaluable* when _____

2. A school might have a long *legacy* of _____
_____

3. Someday I would like to work as an *intern* at _____

4. Parents often *fulfill* a dream when _____

5. *Mobile* libraries, or bookmobiles, are useful because _____
_____

6. It is *evident* that spring is here when _____
_____

7. Teenagers can *cultivate* a healthy lifestyle by _____
_____

8. On city streets, we *control* traffic with _____

9. Benjamin Franklin showed *ingenuity* when he _____

10. You can *assist* elderly neighbors by _____
_____

Challenge Yourself

Write Your Own

Follow the directions to write sentences with the lesson words in italics. Be sure your sentences make sense both grammatically and in meaning.

1. Write a sentence using the word *fulfill*.

2. Write a sentence exactly ten words in length using the word *control*.

3. Write a ten-word sentence using the word *cultivate* in the sixth position.

Word-Solving Strategies:
Context Clues

Embedded Definitions

Sometimes the meaning of a word appears as a phrase right after the word in a text. This is called an embedded definition. Reread this sentence from "Teen Earns $40,000 Science Prize."

> He said that it is evident, or plain to see, that the competitors' "dedication to excellence and passion for math and science will no doubt change the world."

The phrase *plain to see* comes right after the lesson word *evident*. An embedded definition usually follows a comma and may begin with the word *or*.

BE CAREFUL!

Words that appear after a comma may not be a definition.

The contest had many competitors, all of them with excellent math skills.

Here, the words after the comma do not define *competitors*, but tell about their academic talents.

Practice

A. Read the paragraph. Write each highlighted word and its embedded definition in the first two boxes. Then write the meaning of the word.

As a student intern at the natural science museum, Marta worked side-by-side with curators, people in charge of museum exhibits. Marta had tried many extracurricular, or after-school, activities. Clubs and sports were fun, but the museum interested her most. Marta had no qualms, or feelings of doubt or uneasiness, about working with the snakes and lizards in the museum's animal exhibits.

WORD	EMBEDDED DEFINITION	MEANING

B. Write sentences for the highlighted words from the paragraph above. Use an embedded definition in each. You will use one word twice.

1. _____

2. _____

3. _____

4. _____

Practice for Tests

Fill in the bubble next to the answer that best completes the sentence or answers the question.

1. Read this sentence.

   The team will *fulfill* the goal of getting to the finals if it wins this game.

   Fulfill means:
   - ○ **A** meet
   - ○ **B** miss
   - ○ **C** create
   - ○ **D** accept

2. A word closely associated with *ingenuity* is:
   - ○ **A** honesty
   - ○ **B** exaggeration
   - ○ **C** cleverness
   - ○ **D** luck

3. You do NOT *control* a car with the:
   - ○ **A** steering wheel
   - ○ **B** seat belts
   - ○ **C** brakes
   - ○ **D** gas pedal

4. People leave a *legacy* when they:
   - ○ **A** become wealthy
   - ○ **B** have a problem
   - ○ **C** relive the past
   - ○ **D** pass down something

5. The opposite of *evident* is:
   - ○ **A** plain
   - ○ **B** difficult
   - ○ **C** unmistakable
   - ○ **D** unclear

6. Read this sentence.

   My older sister will *intern* at a law office this summer.

   Intern means:
   - ○ **A** volunteer
   - ○ **B** work as a trainee
   - ○ **C** do computer work
   - ○ **D** teach

7. When you *assist*, you do NOT:
   - ○ **A** lend a hand
   - ○ **B** give support
   - ○ **C** get in the way
   - ○ **D** make suggestions

8. You would most likely see a *mobile*:
   - ○ **A** in an art museum
   - ○ **B** on a highway
   - ○ **C** in the water
   - ○ **D** at a hospital

9. You *cultivate land* when you:
   - ○ **A** water it
   - ○ **B** sell it
   - ○ **C** plant in it
   - ○ **D** protect it

10. The opposite of *invaluable* is:
    - ○ **A** valuable
    - ○ **B** worthless
    - ○ **C** precious
    - ○ **D** priceless

Synonyms and Antonyms

In the following Word Bank, you will find synonyms and antonyms for some of the words in Lessons 1–3. (Remember: Some words have both synonyms and antonyms.) Study these words; then complete the exercises below.

demolish	deliver	worthless	develop	gather	introduce
organized	soar	explain	immovable	reconsider	discuss

A. For each sentence, fill in the blank with a SYNONYM for the word in boldface.

1. The leaders of each tribe will meet to **confer** about their common problems and _____ what they should do.

2. The symbols on the ancient stone tablet were hard to **interpret**, but an expert in early languages came in to _____ their mysterious meanings.

3. Students who want to **cultivate** an interest in opera can _____ their love of music by listening to recordings of famous tenors and sopranos.

4. After graduation, Claudio will **reassess** what he'd like to do since he'll have to _____ whether he has enough money to travel or if he needs to get a job.

5. During the holidays, our charity group will _____ food and toys to needy families, but we need volunteers to help **distribute** these items.

B. For each sentence, fill in the blank with an ANTONYM for the word in boldface.

6. Some gardeners favor a **haphazard** planting of different flowers, while others prefer a/an _____ design that looks more formal.

7. Sam thought his baseball card collection was **invaluable**, so after the experts said it was _____ he was stunned.

8. This new X-ray machine is **mobile** and can be brought to remote areas, unlike the older machine that was _____ so patients had to come to it.

9. During the summer, my mother will _____ enough flowers from our garden to make a daily bouquet for the house and **distribute** what is left to our neighbors.

10. The city planners will _____ the buildings the fire destroyed and **reconstruct** new ones.

Word Study: Denotation and Connotation

Every word has a **denotation**, the literal meaning that you find in a dictionary. Many words also have a **connotation**, the feelings and images associated with a word. Connotations are usually described as being positive or negative. A neutral word has no connotations.

POSITIVE	NEGATIVE	NEUTRAL
reach	grab	hold
wealthy	greedy	well-off
chat	gossip	discuss

Look at the word *explanation* in Lesson 1 and some of its synonyms: restatement

analysis   **clarification**   **excuse**

Most of these words are neutral. They have neither positive nor negative connotations. *Excuse*, however, has a negative connotation. It often suggests that someone is giving a reason, which may not be truthful, to explain bad behavior.

Practice

A. Circle the word in parentheses that has the connotation (positive, negative, or neutral) given at the beginning of the sentence.

positive   **1.** This science project shows the (**thinking, originality**) of the students

negative   **2.** The temperature outside is (**hot, sweltering**) today.

negative   **3.** The people (**rioted, demonstrated**) against the new government taxes.

positive   **4.** The (**glaring, glowing**) light brightened the whole room

neutral   **5.** The photographers (**swarmed, gathered**) around the celebrities as they arrived at the premiere.

positive   **6.** The view from the edge of the canyon was (**amazing, surprising**) today.

neutral   **7.** The journalist was (**confined, imprisoned**) until the officer could talk to him.

B. Work with a partner. Write a plus sign (+) if the word has a positive connotation; write a minus sign (−) if the word has a negative connotation. Put a zero (0) if the word is neutral.

1. haphazard ☐   **3.** document ☐   **5.** starving ☐   **7.** praise ☐

2. fulfill ☐   **4.** research ☐   **6.** hypothesis ☐   **8.** excellence ☐

Vocabulary for Comprehension

Read the following passage, in which some of the words you have studied in Lessons 1–3 appear in boldface type. Then answer questions 1–6.

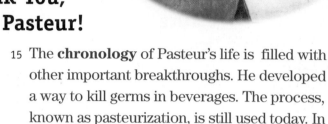

Thank You, Louis Pasteur!

In 1885 a nine-year-old boy named Joseph Meister saw a dog with rabies **approach**. Rabies is a deadly disease spread by the bite of animals. Before Joseph's time, there was little
5 hope for a person bitten by an infected animal. The dog bit Joseph again and again. It was **evident** that Joseph's life was in danger!

Joseph's mother tried to **assess** what had happened and went to Louis Pasteur for help. A
10 French scientist and chemist, Pasteur had done **research** on a vaccine for rabies but had not tried it on humans. Would the vaccine work on Joseph? Pasteur gave Joseph a series of shots. The **invaluable** vaccine saved the boy's life.

15 The **chronology** of Pasteur's life is filled with other important breakthroughs. He developed a way to kill germs in beverages. The process, known as pasteurization, is still used today. In a scientific **debate** over germs, Pasteur proved
20 his **argument** about how germs grow. Pasteur also used his **ingenuity** to save diseased French silkworms and to develop a vaccine for a deadly illness in farm animals.

Pasteur died in 1895. Today his **legacy**
25 continues to make our world a much safer place. Thank you, Louis Pasteur!

1. Something that is **evident** (line 7) is
   ○ **A** uncertain
   ○ **B** plain to see
   ○ **C** hard to understand
   ○ **D** sudden

2. When you do **research** (line 11), you
   ○ **A** think about what you remember
   ○ **B** begin a draft
   ○ **C** make a close study
   ○ **D** make another search

3. Another word for **invaluable** (line 14) in paragraph 2 is
   ○ **A** worthless
   ○ **B** dangerous
   ○ **C** questionable
   ○ **D** priceless

4. A **chronology** (line 15) lists things in
   ○ **A** order of importance
   ○ **B** reverse order
   ○ **C** time order
   ○ **D** alphabetical order

5. In this selection, **argument** (line 20) means
   ○ **A** reason or explanation
   ○ **B** disagreement
   ○ **C** quarrel
   ○ **D** falsehood

6. Someone with **ingenuity** (line 21) can
   ○ **A** predict the future
   ○ **B** solve problems
   ○ **C** work with animals
   ○ **D** work long hours

See the World

LESSON 4

Travels of the Ancient Romans

A modern traveler follows an ancient route and finds surprises along the way.

area	initial	stern
barren	migrate	vicinity
feat	prow	widespread
fraught		

LESSON 5

Why Take Risks to Explore?

Some people risk their lives to explore the unknown.

claim	ransack	transmit
embark	transition	transport
entrust	translate	undertake
prospect		

LESSON 6

Tsunami!

A vacation ends in an unexpected way.

airborne	hemisphere	restrict
atlas	origin	trek
enable	retire	witness
global		

▶ **Watch** a video introduction to this passage at **vocabularyforsuccess.com**.

🔊 **Listen** to this passage at **vocabularyforsuccess.com**.

The Acropolis
Athens, Greece

The Colosseum
Rome, Italy

The Colossus
Rhodes, Turkey

Travels of the Ancient Romans

<travel log>

At the turn of the 21st century, travel writer Tony Perrottet took the type of "vacation" that wealthy people in ancient Rome took 2,000 years ago. In the book that Perrottet wrote about the trip, he described his modern experiences, comparing them to the ancient Romans'. Perrottet's roadmap was a 20-foot-long scroll containing a detailed map of ancient Roman highways. He found this map, as well as a copy of a 2,000-year-old guidebook written for the Romans, at the New York Public Library. As he traveled, Perrottet compared his experiences with what his old guidebook said.

In ancient Rome, the idea of a two-year journey was widespread among wealthy travelers. Perrottet was able to move more quickly, of course. He covered the same vicinity in four months. Surprisingly, though, his trip was like the ancient version in other ways.

Perrottet's journey began in Rome. He followed the Appian Way, the main highway out of the city. Building the Roman highway system was an amazing engineering feat, and the road is still in use today. Perrottet visited other cities in Italy and then went to Greece and Turkey. Like the ancients, Perrottet's tour ended in Egypt with a Nile cruise. Perrottet was amused to read that ancient Romans complained that their tour guides talked too much. He might have said the same thing about the 21st-century guide at the prow of his boat. Perrottet's initial impression had been that small groups of stern

VOCABULARY

widespread	stern
vicinity	barren
feat	migrate
prow	area
initial	fraught

and serious Romans trekked across barren landscapes. However, he learned that Roman tourists traveled in large groups. They tended to migrate in groups from site to site. Perrottet found each tourist area to be fraught with noisy crowds, which is exactly what the old guidebook described. Perrottett was amazed to discover such similarities between his modern trip and journeys taken 2,000 years ago. Not only did Perrottet learn about the people living in these places today, but he also gained a unique understanding of the ancient Romans— the original tourists.

TALK ABOUT IT

With a partner, answer the questions below. Use as many of the highlighted words in the selection as you can.

1. **What are some ways in which Tony Perrottet's *initial* thoughts about ancient travel changed?**

2. **What is another way to describe a *barren* landscape?**

The Nile River Egypt

This ancient map places Rome at the center of the world.

vocabularyforsuccess.com
▶ **Watch** a video introduction for each word
◀)) **Listen** to iWords
📖 **Refer** to the online dictionary

Word Meanings

For each highlighted word on pages 36–37, the meaning is given below. For practice with other meanings, see pages 41–43. For synonyms and antonyms, see page 66.

1. widespread
(WIDE-spred)
(adj.) If an idea has *widespread* approval, many people agree with it.

2. vicinity
(vuh-SIN-i-tee)
(n.) When you are in the *vicinity* of something, you are close to it. If you search the *vicinity* of where you live, you look around your neighborhood.

3. feat
(feet)
(n.) If someone accomplishes something that takes a great deal of courage, effort, or skill, he or she has performed a remarkable *feat*.

4. prow
(prou)
(n.) The *prow* is the pointed front section of a ship or something that sticks out like the front of a ship.

5. initial
(i-NISH-uhl)
(adj.) The first feeling or thought you had as you listened to a new song would be your *initial* impression.

(n.) A person can abbreviate his or her name by using the first letter or *initial*.

6. stern
(sturn)
(adj.) A *stern* expression shows that someone is serious or disapproving.

(n.) The *stern* of a boat is the rear section.

7. barren
(BA-ruhn)
(adj.) A place that is *barren* will not support plant life, so it seems empty.

(adj.) When an animal is described as being *barren*, it cannot produce any offspring.

8. migrate
(MYE-grate)
(v.) People who move from their home country to a faraway location *migrate* from one land to another.

9. area
(AIR-ee-uh)
(n.) An *area* of a park is a section of the park.

(n.) If you calculate the *area* of a shape, you determine the amount of surface within its borders.

10. fraught
(frawt)
(adj.) A journey *fraught* with danger is filled with risk and threat.

Word Talk

Each lesson word has been placed in a category. With a partner, discuss and list items that belong in each category. Compare your results with those of another pair of students.

Initial Reactions When You Hear Bad News	Places Kids Go in the *Vicinity* of School

Widespread Beliefs	Amazing *Feats*	*Barren* Places	Things That Have a *Prow* like a Ship

Situations *Fraught* with Humor	Reasons People Make *Stern* Facial Expressions	*Areas* Where Large Crowds Can Gather	Transportation People Use to *Migrate*

Check for Understanding

Choose the lesson word that completes each sentence. Write the word on the line provided. Some words will be used twice.

area	fraught	stern
barren	initial	vicinity
feat	migrate	widespread
	prow	

1. Tia's grandmother was a/an _____ woman who rarely smiled.

2. Their climb up the mountainside was _____ with challenges and filled with life-threatening risks.

3. During the Gold Rush, many city dwellers chose to _____ west to try to find gold in California.

4. Her _____ comments summarized what she would be speaking about.

5. My kite came down in the _____ of my friends, so they picked it up.

6. The flu was so _____ that nearly half the students were out sick.

7. _____ polls estimated that Ian would win the election when all the votes were counted.

8. One lone tree struggled to survive on the _____, rocky, lifeless hill.

9. The campgrounds are a happy _____, a special place for families to have fun in nature.

10. Kera loved to stand on the ship's _____ and look out over the blue waters of the ocean.

11. Traveling into outer space is an incredible _____ that few people manage to achieve.

12. The _____ field couldn't grow crops because there had been no rain.

Expand Word Meanings

Read the paragraph below to learn other meanings for some of the lesson words.

Thousands of years ago there were no bridges. Sailboats provided the only way to travel great distances across water. But the total area of the sails on these boats was small, so these journeys were slow even when the winds were strong. For warmth, uncomfortable travelers would crowd together in the stern under blankets. Still, ancient tourists sailed to Egypt, often taking animals that they knew were not barren and so could be counted on to reproduce in the new land. Many of these adventurers who made the difficult journey carved their initial in the stones of monuments that had been built along the Nile.

> ! Some of the words from the lesson are used in a different way here. For example, look at *barren*. Here it means "unable to produce offspring." Can you figure out the meanings of the other highlighted words as they are used here? Refer to page 38 to confirm meanings.

Apply Other Meanings

Complete each sentence with a highlighted word from the paragraph above.

1. Many people practice writing their _____ rather than their full name.

2. To find the _____ of a rectangle, multiply the length of one long side by one short side.

3. Since the mare never had any foals, we assumed she was _____.

4. Every sailor knows that the _____ is the back end of a ship.

5. If you want to buy a carpet for your bedroom, you first need to measure the _____ of the floor.

6. The author O. Henry was known for the _____ used in his name.

7. A/An _____ is not pointed because it doesn't have to carve through water.

8. Even though our cat loved kittens, her _____ condition meant that she would never produce any of her own.

9. Our baseball coach had us write the first _____ of our last names in our caps so we would know which hat belonged to which player.

10. The _____ of any circle is determined by multiplying the radius squared by 3.14.

Word Associations

Use what you know about the lesson word in italics to answer each question. Circle the letter next to the phrase that best answers the question. Be prepared to explain your answers.

1. Which reason would cause you to *migrate* from one country to another?

   a. to get away from your ordinary life

   b. to avoid a war or other crisis

   c. to visit a beautiful location

2. Which profession would require you to explore a *barren* place?

   a. farmer

   b. construction worker

   c. astronaut

3. Which of these are you most likely to find on the *prow* of an old ship?

   a. a small carved statue

   b. a sleeping cabin in the stern

   c. the school of fish

4. Which effort might be considered an impressive *feat*?

   a. eating dinner

   b. running a marathon

   c. taking a test

5. Which situation might be described as being *fraught* with danger?

   a. walking the dog

   b. riding a lawn mower

   c. fighting a fire

6. Which of these might you refer to as an *area*?

   a. Earth

   b. the waves on an ocean

   c. the deep end of a pool

7. Which of these would be the *initial* clue that a storm is coming?

   a. dark clouds

   b. rain

   c. a rainbow

8. How can you tell if a person is *stern*?

   a. He smiles.

   b. He looks serious.

   c. He looks nervous.

9. If you were in the *vicinity* of your friend's house, how long might it take you to get there?

   a. one day

   b. five minutes

   c. a few hours

10. What might be described as a *widespread* trend?

    a. the latest fad

    b. an inexpensive treat

    c. a special tool

Check Again

Use what you know about the lesson word in italics to complete each sentence. Be sure your sentences make sense.

1. The cargo was stacked in boxes in the *stern* of the ship because _____

2. If you had just completed an incredible *feat*, you _____

3. As far as we could see, it was a *barren* landscape that _____

4. A disease that is *widespread* would affect _____

5. During the winter, birds *migrate* from _____

6. If there are tornadoes sighted in your *vicinity*, you should _____

7. The *initial* at the top of the page told me that _____

8. We can play in only one *area* of the soccer field because _____

9. The *prow* of the sailboat slammed into the pier _____

10. Walking through the dark forest was an experience *fraught* with mystery because _____

Challenge Yourself

Follow the directions to write sentences with the lesson words in italics. Be sure your sentences make sense both grammatically and in meaning.

1. Write a sentence with the word *barren* in the ninth position.

2. Write a sentence using the word *vicinity* in the seventh position.

3. Write a sentence exactly nine words in length with *stern* in the fifth position.

Word-Solving Strategies: Context Clues

Restatement/Synonyms

Readers can understand unfamiliar words by finding a nearby word with a similar meaning or a phrase that explains the word. Reread this sentence from "Travels of the Ancient Romans."

> Perrottet's initial impression had been that small groups of stern and serious Romans trekked across barren landscapes.

Notice that along with the word *stern*, the author describes Romans as *serious*. If there are no context clues to help you figure out a word's meaning, consult an Internet dictionary.

Some words in the same sentence as an unknown word may have different meanings. Read this sentence:

> *Romans wanted to visit exotic and crowded locations.*

The adjective *exotic* describes something that is interesting because it's foreign. Here, "and" does not mean that *exotic* is the same as *crowded*.

BE CAREFUL!

Practice

A. Write a highlighted vocabulary word and its synonym in the first two boxes. Use context clues to write another meaning in the third box.

There are many challenges to world travel. Understanding local customs can be difficult because foreign traditions are often so different from your own. You arrive at a bus depot or railroad station and have to use coins that often aren't the same size as yours. The money often pictures dignitaries, or important citizens, who are unknown to you. Language can be a problem, too. Travelers have to convey what they want by communicating with unfamiliar words. Local people may accommodate you by helping to translate.

WORD	SYNONYM	WORD MEANING

B. Write a sentence for each of the highlighted words from the paragraph above. Include a synonym for each word.

1. _____

2. _____

3. _____

4. _____

Practice for Tests

Fill in the bubble next to the answer that best completes the sentence or answers the question.

1. Read this sentence.

   The interactions of these two friends were *fraught* with conflict.

   Fraught means:
   - A often filled
   - B usually empty
   - C rarely completed
   - D avoided carefully

2. The opposite of *initial* is:
   - A original
   - B first
   - C honest
   - D last

3. When you *migrate*, you do NOT:
   - A travel a long distance
   - B leave a place completely
   - C plan to go back soon
   - D find a new home

4. In which of these places could the *area* be accurately measured?
   - A a football field
   - B a riverbank
   - C a mountain range
   - D outer space

5. A *widespread* rumor would:
   - A travel very slowly
   - B be hard to believe
   - C be frequently repeated
   - D be about people you knew

6. Read this sentence.

   The *prow* of the snowplow was shaped like a triangle to part the deep snow.

   Prow means:
   - A height
   - B side
   - C top
   - D tip

7. You refer to an effort as a *feat* when:
   - A it is something you cannot do
   - B you are impressed by it
   - C you have never heard of it
   - D it is something many others do

8. A place is said to be *barren* if:
   - A it is just rocks and soil
   - B it is hard to explore
   - C no children ever go there
   - D it has changed greatly over time

9. An explosive noise occurring in your *vicinity* would most likely:
   - A turn your head slowly
   - B force you to strain to hear it
   - C make you cover your ears
   - D wonder what the sound was

10. A word closely associated with *stern* is:
    - A front
    - B harsh
    - C angry
    - D obvious

LESSON
5

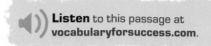
Why Take Risks to Explore?

<persuasive essay>

Exploring the unknown can be dangerous, but people want to see and learn new things. In the 15th and 16th centuries, European explorers chose to embark on journeys to discover new worlds. Those voyages required travel across oceans in search of trade routes, gold and other wealth, or lands to claim for their home country. Life at sea was difficult and it was not always possible to transport fresh food or drinking water. Pirates might attack and ransack the explorers' ships. Still, crew members chose to entrust their lives to the leaders of these explorations. Why would individuals want to undertake such extraordinary risks?

The answer is that these explorers made important discoveries. They were also able to transmit their ideas and ways of living to people in faraway places. Those early explorations led to the gradual transition to a different way of life for the people of the New World. If these adventurous explorers of the past had not left home, our nation as we know it might not exist today.

Modern-day space explorers are risk-takers as well. Since the middle of the 20th century, astronauts have explored an enormous and unknown world—outer space. There are risks in space, just as on Earth. In fact, several astronauts have lost their lives in tragic accidents. Yet, their courage has helped NASA to send others into space, where they have walked on the surface of the Moon and lived and worked on the International Space Station, 250 miles above Earth.

Explorers must be willing to take risks. Think of what we would not know about the world if the prospect of danger had kept these adventurers at home. True explorers are individuals who translate their dreams into reality. They board ships and space shuttles because they are willing to risk the unknown, without letting fear get in their way.

TALK ABOUT IT

With a partner, answer the questions below. Use as many of the highlighted words in the selection as you can.

1. What makes some people willing to *undertake* risks in order to explore?

2. Would you be willing to *embark* on a risky exploration? Why or why not?

vocabularyforsuccess.com
▶ **Watch** a video introduction for each word
◀)) **Listen** to iWords
📖 **Refer** to the online dictionary

Word Meanings

For each highlighted word on pages 46–47, the meaning is given below. For practice with other meanings, see pages 51–53. For synonyms and antonyms, see page 66.

1. embark
(em-BARK)

(v.) When you board a vehicle to begin a journey, you *embark* on a trip. When you start something new, you *embark* on it.

2. claim
(klaym)

(v.) When you *claim* something, you state you own or have the right to it.

(n.) A *claim* is a demand to get money that you believe you are due, such as filing an insurance *claim* when something has been stolen.

3. transport
(tranz-PORT)

(v.) When you carry or move something from one place to another, you *transport* it.

4. ransack
(RAN-sak)

(v.) When you search through your own or someone else's possessions thoroughly, you *ransack* them, often creating a mess with the items.

5. entrust
(en-TRUHST)

(v.) When you *entrust* a friend to hold money for you, you are confident that he will keep it safe and give it back to you.

6. undertake
(uhn-dur-TAKE)

(v.) When you take on an assignment or set out to do something, you *undertake* it.

7. transmit
(tranz-MIT)

(v.) When you *transmit* something to another person, you send or give it.

8. transition
(tran-ZISH-uhn)

(n.) Middle school is a *transition* between elementary school and high school.

(v.) Children who no longer need training wheels *transition* from four wheels to two.

9. prospect
(PROSS-pekt)

(n.) If you are excited by the *prospect,* or promise, of something that will happen in the future, you look forward to it.

(v.) When you dig in the ground looking for precious metal, you *prospect* for minerals.

10. translate
(TRANZ-late)

(v.) You *translate* something when you change it from one form to another, such as when you *translate* a summer job into more spending money.

(v.) When you take words in one language and change them to words in another language, you *translate* from one language to another.

48

Word Talk

Each lesson word is listed here. With a partner, take turns drawing a picture to illustrate the meaning of six of the words. As one partner draws, the other partner identifies the vocabulary word.

claim (v.)

embark

entrust

prospect (n.)

ransack

transition (n.)

translate

transmit

transport

undertake

ransack

Check for Understanding

Choose the lesson word that completes each sentence. Write the word on the line provided. Some words will be used twice.

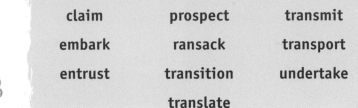

claim	prospect	transmit
embark	ransack	transport
entrust	transition	undertake
	translate	

1. Tonight the raccoons may _____ the garbage bags and make a mess.

2. Father wants to _____ on our trip early, so we will leave at dawn.

3. Our English teacher showed us how to _____ our feelings into poems.

4. Keisha's _____ from country to city was complete when she stopped wearing cowboy boots and began wearing shoes.

5. Olivia knew she could _____ Rosa with her secret.

6. The _____ of making more money in the future made Zack happy today.

7. We used wheelbarrows to _____ rocks that were too heavy to carry.

8. The class will _____, not avoid, the challenge the principal has given.

9. The baseball team is better than ever and hopes to _____ the title of best athletic group in the school.

10. If a thief were to _____ Leon's room, it couldn't get any messier.

11. They will use a truck, a train, and a ship to _____ their products abroad.

12. "_____ your message now," Vera said, "so we can get a reply back from them very soon."

Expand Word Meanings

Read the paragraph below to learn other meanings for some of the lesson words.

One day my uncle found a treasure map in an old book. He asked me to translate its Spanish notes into English. The map pointed to a spot on public land. Uncle Bob went to the authorities to make a claim. The mayor said that if we found treasure, it would be ours. After we got permission, we began to prospect for gold. Lazy Uncle Bob read the map while we kids did the digging. It was sad how quickly we managed to transition from excited miners to disappointed workers. If we found gold, we'd have been wealthy. Instead, we just got tired and stuck in an empty hole!

> **!** If you know one meaning of a word, you can usually determine another. If you *prospect*, you are acting as a *prospector* who digs in the ground with the *prospect*, or possibility, of finding treasure there. Review the other highlighted words to see how verbs become nouns and nouns become verbs.

Apply Other Meanings

Complete each sentence with a highlighted word from the paragraph above.

1. Some skaters find it difficult to _____ from ice skates to roller blades, because skating on ice requires different skills than skating on the street.

2. Even though we didn't know French, my family could _____ restaurant menus in Paris because there were pictures showing us what the unfamiliar words meant.

3. Jenna's camera stopped working so she filed a _____ with the camera store.

4. Tourists _____ around old silver mines looking for treasure that was overlooked.

5. As fall approaches, students and teachers often find it exciting to _____ from summer break to the start of school.

6. It is hard to _____ the word *war* into a language that does not have a word for *fighting*.

7. After the fire, our insurance _____ included lost clothing, books, shoes, and art.

8. Many older adults perfer writing with a pen and paper rather than using a computer, because they can't _____ to another way of communicating.

9. If you lose your job, you can file a _____ and receive unemployment benefits.

10. Our guide failed to _____ the sign properly, and we ended up lost in a foreign city.

Word Associations

Use what you know about the lesson word in italics to answer each question. Circle the letter next to the phrase that best answers the question. Be prepared to explain your answers.

1. Which item could a person *transport* from place to place?

    a. a mountain range

    b. a large-screen TV

    c. a firmly held belief

2. Which of these can a person *translate*?

    a. fruit from another country

    b. a new bicycle

    c. a Russian song

3. Which is a place you cannot *prospect*?

    a. the sky

    b. a mountain

    c. a riverbed

4. Which of these might a person *entrust* to a close friend?

    a. their name

    b. a favorite shirt

    c. a sandwich

5. What would be the best way to *transmit* a message?

    a. keep it to yourself

    b. write it down

    c. send an e-mail

6. Why would a burglar decide to *ransack* a house?

    a. to run outside and get away

    b. to hide evidence of a crime

    c. to find hidden valuables quickly

7. Where are you when you *embark* on a trip?

    a. at the beginning of it

    b. in the middle of it

    c. at the end of it

8. What would a person be likely to *claim* as his or her own?

    a. blame for a problem

    b. the idea for an invention

    c. something they want to buy

9. Which of these people would be likely to *undertake* a long-term project?

    a. a person with no extra time

    b. a young person

    c. an impatient person

10. How would you *transition* between an old home and a new one?

    a. by changing habits gradually

    b. by refusing to try anything new

    c. by ignoring where you came from

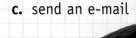

Check Again

Use what you know about the lesson word in italics to complete each sentence. Be sure your sentences make sense.

1. When you decide to *undertake* a long journey, you should consider _____
_____

2. During the *transition* from winter to spring, _____

3. When you *entrust* someone with your valuables, you expect _____

4. If thieves were to break into your house and *ransack* it, you would _____
_____

5. If you were facing the *prospect* of a hurricane in your area, you might _____
_____

6. When you *claim* you are a great singer, you should be willing to _____

7. When a tourist tries to *translate* a word from his own language to another, he _____
_____

8. To *transport* a load of firewood from the forest, you might _____

9. There are many ways to *transmit* messages to your friends, so _____
_____

10. If you were about to *embark* on a trip, your family and friends would _____

Challenge Yourself

Follow the directions to write sentences with the lesson words in italics. Be sure your sentences make sense both grammatically and in meaning.

1. Write a sentence with the word *transport* in the third position.

2. Write a sentence exactly ten words in length with *claim* in the fourth position.

3. Write a question with the word *entrust* in the fifth position.

Word-Solving Strategies: Prefixes

The prefix trans-: "across," "on or to the other side"

Prefixes add meaning to a root word by combining the meaning of the prefix with the meaning of the root word. A prefix like *trans-*, taken from Latin and meaning "across," "beyond," or "on or to the other side," brings new meanings to other root words.

As an example, the word *transport* from this lesson combines the meaning of "across" with the meaning of the Latin root word *portare*, meaning "to carry." We see this root in other English words, such as *portable* and *porter*. To transport something is to carry it from one location to another or across a body of water.

Another word from this lesson, *transmit*, is similar. In Latin, *mittere* means "to send." Again, the meaning of *across* extends the meaning of *send* so that *transmit* means "send across."

For each of the *trans-* words in this lesson, the extended meaning of "across," "beyond," or "on or to the other side" combines with a Latin root word to expand the meaning of the new word.

Transition is a form of *transit* meaning "to go across," while *translate* means "to carry across" or "change from one form to another."

Examples

Study these examples of root words combined with the prefix *trans-*:

act → transact
fusion → transfusion
lucent (light) → translucent
figure → transfigure
fix → transfix
scribe (write) → transcribe

BE CAREFUL!

Because the word *trans-* in Latin is a preposition, it was combined with verbs to form new verbs. Therefore, the root word of *transit* is not *it*. The verb *transire* is the root that has come down to us as our verb *transit*, both meaning "to go across." The Latin verb *transferre* became *translater* in Anglo-French and has become our word *translate*.

Practice

Use what you've learned about the prefix *trans-* to create new words from root words by adding *trans-*.

1. action _____

2. Atlantic _____

3. form _____

4. continental _____

5. script _____

6. plant _____

7. mission _____

8. pose _____

Practice for Tests

Fill in the bubble next to the answer that best completes the sentence or answers the question.

1. Read this sentence:

   Cell phones *transmit* signals to towers that then pass the signals to satellites.

   Transmit means:
   ○ **A** send
   ○ **B** launch
   ○ **C** improve
   ○ **D** receive

2. When ships *embark* at dawn, they:
   ○ **A** stop
   ○ **B** sink
   ○ **C** dock
   ○ **D** leave

3. The opposite of *claim* is:
   ○ **A** demand
   ○ **B** want
   ○ **C** deny
   ○ **D** request

4. In which list do all items *transport* people?
   ○ **A** taxi, stagecoach, hot air balloon
   ○ **B** ocean liner, luggage, train
   ○ **C** bus, passenger, terminal
   ○ **D** horse, sailboat, port

5. A word associated with *prospect* is:
   ○ **A** sunset
   ○ **B** memory
   ○ **C** anticipation
   ○ **D** eyesight

6. Read this sentence:

   The volunteers will *undertake* a project to clean up litter.

   Undertake means:
   ○ **A** finish up
   ○ **B** give away
   ○ **C** start planning
   ○ **D** take on

7. You *translate* if you:
   ○ **A** carry something to a place
   ○ **B** convert one thing to another
   ○ **C** make something happen quickly
   ○ **D** show how two things are related

8. When you *entrust* people with something, you believe they will NOT:
   ○ **A** lose it
   ○ **B** protect it
   ○ **C** hide it
   ○ **D** return it

9. You would most likely *transition*:
   ○ **A** among a group of friends
   ○ **B** while doing one activity
   ○ **C** between two schools
   ○ **D** without much effect on you

10. If thieves *ransack* a house, they:
   ○ **A** organize it
   ○ **B** search it
   ○ **C** destroy it
   ○ **D** confuse it

▶ **Watch** a video introduction to this passage at vocabularyforsuccess.com.

🔊 **Listen** to this passage at vocabularyforsuccess.com.

Visitors and residents crowd the streets and markets of Thailand before the 2004 Tsunami.

Tsunami!

<online feature article>

Open an atlas to a map of any continent in the world, and there is a good chance that Kira Coonley has been there. This young American is a global traveler. One of her most memorable travel experiences took place in Asia.

In 2004, Coonley traveled through Thailand. She started out in the northern part of the country, where she stayed in the crowded city of Chiang Mai. In this Asian city, she looked different from the people around her because of her American origin. Coonley tried to blend in, eating the spicy foods and speaking Thai. However she felt that her identity would always restrict her to the status of a foreigner.

That December, Coonley journeyed to the southern part of Thailand. She traveled by boat and overnight bus, then made a trek on foot to Ton Sai beach for the restful last part of her trip.

One morning, Coonley felt a gentle tremor. Everything around her seemed normal, though. Workers had begun their day. Store owners were opening their shops. Beachgoers were sitting out towels as usual, ready to retire in the sand for a few hours in the sun.

At breakfast, Coonley saw the tide recede very rapidly. Suddenly, an enormous wave appeared and swept away everything in its path. It was a tsunami! Coonley and others quickly ran to higher ground for safety. They had no idea of how much destruction they would witness in the low-lying area below.

VOCABULARY

atlas	retire
global	witness
origin	enable
restrict	hemisphere
trek	airborne

The survivors of the tsunami comforted each other. They had been strangers before. Now they were united in their shock and grief. Kira Coonley's experience would enable her to understand that, in times of disaster and pain, differences among people don't mean anything. Days later, she left the Eastern Hemisphere and went home. Yet within two weeks she was airborne once again—returning to Thailand. She wanted to help rebuild the country that was so devastated by the tsunami.

A view of the wreckage of Ton Sai Bay in Thailand after the 2004 tsunami

TALK ABOUT IT

With a partner, answer the questions below. Use as many of the highlighted words in the selection as you can.

1. What did Kira Coonley's tsunami experience *enable* her to understand?

2. What can people learn from *global* travels?

vocabularyforsuccess.com

▶ **Watch** a video introduction for each word

◀)) **Listen** to iWords 🎧

📖 **Refer** to the online dictionary

Word Meanings

For each highlighted word on pages 56–57, the meaning is given below.
For practice with other meanings, see pages 61–63. For synonyms and
antonyms, see page 66.

1. atlas
(AT-luhss)

(n.) When maps or charts are bound into a book, it is called an *atlas*.

(n.) A person who is able to deal with a heavy burden is called an
Atlas, often jokingly, in honor of the god from Greek mythology who
supported the heavens on his shoulders.

2. global
(GLOHB-uhl)

(adj.) Something that is *global* relates to, or is found in, mulitiple places all
over the world.

3. origin
(OR-i-jin)

(n.) The place where you come from or where you started is your *origin*.

4. restrict
(ree-STRIKT)

(v.) When you *restrict* something, you keep it held back or restrained inside
of boundaries.

5. trek
(trek)

(n.) Any long, difficult journey is known as a *trek*.

(v.) When you *trek* across a large region, such as the Great Plains, you
experience a challenging journey.

6. retire
(ree-TIRE)

(v.) When you step away from the action or relax, you *retire* to a calmer place.

(v.) When you stop working for a living, you *retire* from the workforce.

7. witness
(WIT-niss)

(v.) By seeing or experiencing something that happens, you *witness*
it occurring.

(n.) A person who sees something happen is a *witness*. A *witness* might tell
about what he or she saw in a court of law.

8. enable
(i-NAY-buhl)

(v.) When you make it possible for something
to happen, you *enable* it. For example, when
you help someone, you *enable* her by making
it easier for her to do something.

9. hemisphere
(hem-uhss-fihr)

(n.) Half of the planet Earth or any sphere is
a *hemisphere*.

10. airborne
(AIR-born)

(adj.) Something that is up in the sky or being
carried by an aircraft is *airborne*.

Word Talk

Each lesson word has been placed in a category. With a partner, discuss and list items that belong in each category. Compare your results with those of another pair of students.

Airborne Things	Things You Would Carry on a *Trek*

Products Whose *Origin* Is a Cow	Ways to *Enable* a New Student's Acceptance	Countries in the Southern *Hemisphere*	Places Where You Can *Retire* After School

Global Concerns	Reasons to Look in an *Atlas*	Items That *Restrict* Movement	Events You Could *Witness*

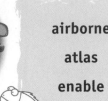

LESSON 6

Check for Understanding

Choose the lesson word that completes each sentence. Write the word on the line provided. Some words will be used twice.

airborne	global	retire
atlas	hemisphere	trek
enable	origin	witness
	restrict	

1. The long _____ from the East Coast to California by wagon trains took months.

2. When it's winter below the equator, it is summer in the Northern _____.

3. My town doesn't _____ what people can recycle, so we put plastic, newspaper, metal, and glass in our bins.

4. In a world _____, you can see where the Mississippi River ends.

5. Many products are sold in American stores, but their _____ is foreign.

6. A larger air tank will _____ a scuba diver to stay underwater longer.

7. _____ satellite systems allow you to find out where you are on the planet.

8. If you lived in the White House, you would _____ many historical events just by watching what happened around you.

9. We like to _____ in the shade after leaving the intense heat of the beach.

10. Our kites stayed _____ until the wind died down.

11. My teacher held the globe and ran her finger along the line that divided one _____ from the other.

12. A(n) _____ contains information in addition to pictures of maps.

Expand Word Meanings

Read the paragraph below to learn other meanings for some of the lesson words.

When we think of hiking, most of us imagine a pleasant stroll through the woods. But more and more people seem to like hiking through New York City. Lots of visitors trek from one end of the island to the other in all kinds of weather. I've been a witness to this trend. I've seen these hikers carrying all the supplies and gear they need. And many arrange to meet up with fellow hikers at one of the city's famous tourist attractions. The giant brass statue of Atlas at Rockefeller Center is one example. My great aunt, who will soon retire and have more free time, can't wait to go on this grand adventure herself. And I can't wait to join her.

> **!** Notice the connection between the meanings of *atlas* as a book and *Atlas* as a strong person. Statues of Atlas, the Greek Titan, showed him supporting the heavens. The sky was shown as a sphere, which looked like Earth, so maps of every place on Earth became associated with Atlas.

Apply Other Meanings

Complete each sentence with a highlighted word from the paragraph above.

1. After the car accident, I served as a/an _____, telling the police exactly what I saw.

2. My friend proved herself to be a real _____ when she took on the burden of choreographing the school musical.

3. Skiers in the mountains will _____ from resort to resort for weeks as a test of strength and skiing ability.

4. My grandfather didn't _____ until he was eighty because he liked working

5. My father is like a/an _____ who often takes on others' problems as well as his own.

6. It is never too early to start saving money for when you _____ because you won't be earning a salary then.

7. Dimitri cannot testify as a/an _____ in court because he didn't see what happened.

8. The journey from my house to yours required me to _____ twenty-six miles.

9. Father isn't really going to _____ completely, since he'll still work part-time.

10. The _____ brought photos with her to prove what she had seen.

Word Associations

Use what you know about the lesson word in italics to answer each question. Circle the letter next to the phrase that best answers the question. Be prepared to explain your answers.

1. Which of these could serve as a *witness* to an event?

   a. a duck
   b. a child
   c. a mirror

2. Which of the following is a real *trek*?

   a. a half-mile jog
   b. a mall walk every day
   c. a hike through the rain forest

3. Which action is most likely to have *global* effects?

   a. voting for U.S. President
   b. voting for student council president
   c. voting for teacher of the year in your school district

4. Which of these objects has a shape similar to a *hemisphere*?

   a. a full balloon
   b. an open umbrella
   c. a highway exit

5. Which of these devices would *enable* you to communicate better?

   a. a cell phone
   b. a television
   c. a map

6. Which feature would you find in an *atlas*?

   a. biographies of world leaders
   b. lyrics to popular songs
   c. symbols showing mountains

7. Which of these items might stay *airborne*?

   a. a plastic bag
   b. a swimming pool
   c. an automobile

8. Which of these would most likely be the *origin* of a movie script?

   a. an expensive camera
   b. a best-selling novel
   c. a popular actor

9. Which of the following could *restrict* your vision?

   a. eyeglasses
   b. a blindfold
   c. sunlight

10. Which piece of furniture would you *retire* in after a hard day?

    a. a hammock
    b. a table
    c. a refrigerator

Check Again

Use what you know about the lesson word in italics to complete each sentence. Be sure your sentences make sense.

1. After a long *trek* through the mountains, your feet _____

2. To *enable* a person with a broken foot to get around, _____

3. If you live in the Northern *Hemisphere*, in the summer you _____

4. In order to *restrict* people from entering a room, you can _____

5. When people *retire*, their lives change because _____
_____

6. If you are trying to understand the *origin* of a word, you _____
_____

7. A kite that is *airborne* can _____

8. If you were to *witness* an incredible sporting event, you'd want to _____
_____

9. During a *global* search for a criminal, the police would look _____
_____

10. If you look in an *atlas*, you can find _____
_____

Challenge Yourself

Write Your Own

Follow the directions to write sentences with the lesson words in italics. Be sure your sentences make sense both grammatically and in meaning.

1. Write a sentence with the word *atlas* in the fifth position.

2. Write a sentence of exactly six words in length using the word *witness*.

3. Write a question with the word *retire* in the sixth position.

Word-Solving Strategies: Context Clues

Examples

Sometimes authors define an unknown word with an example of the word's meaning. The meaning might be in the same sentence or in nearby sentences. Reread this sentence from "Tsunami!"

> Open an atlas to a map of any continent in the world, and there is a good chance that Kira Coonley has been there.

Notice that right after the word **atlas** the author has included an example of what is found in an **atlas**: *a map of any continent in the world.*

BE CAREFUL!

> Information that follows an unknown word may not be an example of its meaning.
>
> *Kira's trek began with a difficult bike ride.*
>
> If you do not know the word *trek*, you might assume it had something to do with a difficult bike ride, instead of a lengthy journey.

Practice

A. Write a highlighted word and an example in the first two boxes. Use context clues to write another meaning for the word in the third box.

With only three people per acre, Australia has the capacity to support a much larger population on its 76 million square acres. All that land contains many environments. The deserts of the Outback are famously beautiful. There are few water reservoirs in the Outback, but the rain forests of Victoria have many lakes and rivers. Eighty-five percent of Australia's plants and mammals are exclusive to the continent—especially marsupials, which are rare anywhere else. This one statistic shows why Australia is special.

WORD	EXAMPLE	WORD MEANING

B. Write sentences using two of the highlighted words from the paragraph above. Include an example that explains the word meanings.

1. _____

_____

2. _____

_____

Practice for Tests

Fill in the bubble next to the answer that best completes the sentence or answers the question.

1. Read this sentence.

   After playing basketball every day, Tonya goes to her room to *retire*.

   Retire means:

   ○ **A** relax
   ○ **B** work out
   ○ **C** clean up
   ○ **D** be alone

2. When you *witness* something, you can:
   ○ **A** change or affect its outcome
   ○ **B** make it disappear
   ○ **C** change the way it happened
   ○ **D** describe your experience

3. The opposite of *enable* is:
   ○ **A** tackle
   ○ **B** help
   ○ **C** prevent
   ○ **D** enrage

4. In which group can all the items be described as practically *global*?
   ○ **A** shipping routes, English, birds
   ○ **B** sea currents, a path, dreams
   ○ **C** a bridge, the Internet, holidays
   ○ **D** the U.N., local climate, airlines

5. A word closely associated with *origin* is:
   ○ **A** destination
   ○ **B** home
   ○ **C** beginning
   ○ **D** travel

6. Read this sentence.

   The brain's right *hemisphere* controls the muscles on the body's left side.

   Hemisphere means

   ○ **A** bone
   ○ **B** fold
   ○ **C** section
   ○ **D** half

7. You would use an *atlas* to:
   ○ **A** lift weights in the gym
   ○ **B** find Berlin on a map of Germany
   ○ **C** see buildings in Berlin, Germany
   ○ **D** see images of Earth from space

8. When you *restrict* someone, you:
   ○ **A** hold him back
   ○ **B** make him go back to the start
   ○ **C** release him
   ○ **D** make him obey you

9. You would most likely be on a *trek* if you were:
   ○ **A** watching TV
   ○ **B** swimming in a large pool
   ○ **C** walking a long distance
   ○ **D** getting a ride to school

10. Something that is *airborne* would:
    ○ **A** bounce
    ○ **B** fly
    ○ **C** skid
    ○ **D** splash

Synonyms and Antonyms

In the following Word Bank, you will find synonyms and antonyms for some of the words in Lessons 4–6. (Remember: Some words have both synonyms and antonyms.) Study these words; then complete the exercises below.

| local | work | productive | board | allow | release |
| tidy | first | facilitate | popular | business | send |

A. For each sentence, fill in the blank with a SYNONYM for the word in boldface.

1. For many immigrants, their initial **glimpse** of America was the Statue of Liberty, a sight that dominated their _____ memories of life in their new country.

2. The counselor explained that as soon as the counselors _____ the sailboat, they would **embark** on the adventure of their lives.

3. Even though the government would not permit the news media to **transmit** information through television or radio, the protesters used cell phones to _____ pictures and words.

4. Grandpa's financial plan will **enable** his grandchildren to attend college and will _____ them to focus on their education rather than on money.

5. There was a **widespread** belief during the 1800s that you could get rich panning for gold because the idea of great wealth was _____ at the time.

B. For each sentence, fill in the blank with an ANTONYM for the word in boldface.

6. Although a dozen workers chose to **retire** this year, others continued to _____ for our production team.

7. If a bear came to **ransack** your camp, it would take hours to make the site _____.

8. The land at the farm was **barren** at first, but after we added organic matter, the soil became quite _____.

9. Park officials had to _____ their wild animals from a fenced-in area used to **restrict** their movements.

10. Once the disease was **widespread** and discovered overseas, all hope of keeping it _____ disappeared.

Word Study: Idioms

When someone says "I'm all ears," he doesn't really mean he's covered with ears. He means that he is listening attentively. "I'm all ears" is an example of an **idiom**, or a phrase that means something different from the literal meaning of its words.

Many of the words in Lessons 4–6 have meanings that can be expressed as idioms. You might say when you want to *retire* (Lesson 6) for the night that you are ready to "hit the hay." You really mean that you are going to bed to sleep and not that you have hay in your room that you plan to hit.

Practice

Read each sentence. Use context clues to figure out the meaning of each idiom in boldface. Then, write the letter of the definition for the idiom.

_____ 1. Marta knew that her report needed a **fresh pair of eyes**, so she asked her sister to read it before handing it in.

_____ 2. When Abe kept interrupting Jack's plan with his own ideas, Jack accused him of being a **backseat driver**.

_____ 3. No matter how many problems she has, Jasmine always seems to **land on her feet**.

_____ 4. The company meeting was so confusing, it was clear that the **right hand didn't know what the left hand was doing**.

_____ 5. As Kayden watched his team score another run, he wondered if the opposing team was ready to **say uncle**.

_____ 6. Micki **missed the boat** when she was late turning in her application.

a. succeed when failure is more than likely

b. admit defeat

c. a person who offers unwanted or wrong advice regarding a task that another person is doing

d. a person looking at something that he or she has never seen before

e. didn't take advantage of an opportunity

f. severe lack of communication

g. leave when things get hard

Apply

Work with a partner to find out the meaning of each idiom. (Use an online or print dictionary.) Then work together to write a sentence for each item.

1. hit the road

2. hit a nerve

3. take the fall

4. walking on air

5. keep your cool

6. take the wind out of his sails

7. hit the books

8. back to square one

Vocabulary for Comprehension

Read the following passage, in which some of the words you have studied in Lessons 4–6 appear in boldface type. Then answer questions 1–6.

Record-Setting Row

A 22-year-old woman accomplished a **feat** that no other American can **claim**. Katie Spotz rowed across the Atlantic Ocean alone, the youngest person ever to do so. She used a
5 specially built, covered rowboat to **transport** herself from Africa to South America. The boat measured 19 feet from its **prow** to its **stern**. Spotz packed enough food for 110 days. The journey took 70 days to cover 2,817 miles of
10 open ocean. Spotz had to row 400 miles out of her way at the very end. High winds and strong currents forced her to detour from a course **fraught** with danger.

At one point, a small fire in one of her **global**
15 positioning systems threatened her safety.

Luckily, it was only the GPS she used to **transmit** her location all over the world to readers of her blog. Spotz avoided nasty storms as she rowed across a section of Earth's
20 Northern **Hemisphere**. She watched dolphins and sharks swim by, and birds rested beside her. She arrived with her hands covered in calluses from rowing eight to ten hours a day.

Spotz was no stranger to adventure. Before
25 rowing, she decided to **undertake** other challenges. She swam the length of the Allegheny River and rode a bicycle across the United States.

1. A person who accomplishes a **feat** (line 1) has
   - A injured a part of his leg
   - B performed a task
   - C raised a lot of money
   - D done something difficult

2. In line 7, **prow** means
   - A front tip
   - B left side
   - C top of the sail
   - D cabin and mast

3. Another term for **fraught** (line 13) is
   - A full of
   - B stripped
   - C threatened
   - D confused by

4. An example of something **global** (line 14) is
   - A Atlantic Ocean currents
   - B the Allegheny River
   - C a bike ride across America
   - D airline travel to other continents

5. When you **transmit** (line 17), you
   - A change it to your language
   - B carry to the end
   - C communicate to others
   - D read out loud

6. Something that you do NOT **undertake** (line 25) would be
   - A something that is easy
   - B something you plan well
   - C something you refuse to do
   - D something you can do

Natural Disasters

LESSON 7

Surviving an Earthquake

Knowing what to do during a natural disaster could save your life.

achievable	invariable	mantle
alter	jolt	obtainable
collide	landscape	signal
crust		

LESSON 8

Hurricane Hunters

Learn about the men and women who risk their lives to keep us safe.

aerial	cycle	hardship
atmosphere	despite	ordeal
challenge	expand	source
climate		

LESSON 9

The Great Flood

See the devastating effects of the United States' worst flood disaster.

barrier	erosion	mass
buoy	inaccessible	risk
debris	incapable	vessel
deluge		

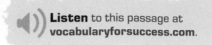

▶ **Watch** a video introduction to this passage at **vocabularyforsuccess.com**.

🔊 **Listen** to this passage at **vocabularyforsuccess.com**.

Surviving an Earthquake

<how-to article>

When a powerful earthquake hit Haiti in January 2010, it killed approximately 230,000 people. Weeks later, Chile experienced an earthquake 500 times more powerful. About 500 people died there. Many factors, including where the earthquakes struck, contributed to these uneven death tolls. One important difference between the two events was that in 2010, the people of Chile were better prepared. In 1960 they experienced the most powerful earthquake ever. That was a signal to the government that another huge quake might follow. The result was that the people of Chile learned the how-tos of earthquake survival.

The three keys to earthquake survival are drop, cover, and hold on. It's important to think fast when you feel the first jolt. If you are in bed, stay there and put a pillow over your head. If you are anywhere else, drop to the floor, and take cover under the nearest piece of furniture. That way, falling objects will collide with a desk or table, not you. Then hold on tight. An invariable rule is to never run outside during an earthquake. However, if you are already outside, safety is obtainable by moving to an open space as quickly as possible.

In addition to individual know-how, the government of Chile decided that building better structures would make greater safety achievable. The earth's crust and mantle—the layer below the crust—form a skin. It is made up of many plates that move and slide over each other. Sometimes, however, the plates' rough edges get stuck on each other. When the plates finally do move, the pressure that is

This building in Port-au-Prince, Haiti, was destroyed by the devastating earthquake of 2010.

~VOCABULARY~

signal	achievable
jolt	crust
collide	mantle
invariable	alter
obtainable	landscape

released causes extreme shaking. Engineers in Chile studied how to design buildings that were likely to withstand such shaking, and the government required new buildings to follow those designs. No one can predict exactly when and where an earthquake will occur or how it will alter the landscape, but knowing what you and your community can do will help people survive.

TALK ABOUT IT

With a partner, answer the questions below. Use as many of the highlighted words in the selection as you can.

1. How might an earthquake *alter* the *landscape* in a town?

2. What should people do if they feel the first *jolt* of an earthquake?

A more powerful, but less deadly, earthquake later occurred in Chile.

LESSON 7

Word Meanings

vocabularyforsuccess.com
▶ **Watch** a video introduction for each word
◀)) **Listen** to iWords
📖 **Refer** to the online dictionary

For each highlighted word on pages 70–71, the meaning is given below. For practice with other meanings, see pages 75–77. For synonyms and antonyms, see page 100.

1. signal
(SIG-nuhl)

(n.) A *signal* is something that gives notice or warning.

(v.) When something communicates or is a sign of something that is about to happen, it is said to *signal* the event.

2. jolt
(johlt)

(n.) A *jolt* is a sudden sharp, jerky movement.

(v.) When you *jolt* something, you move it with a quick or hard blow.

3. collide
(kuh-LIDE)

(v.) When things crash into one another, they *collide*.

4. invariable
(in-VAIR-ee-uh-buhl)

(adj.) Something that is *invariable* does not change and cannot change.

5. obtainable
(uhb-TAIN-uh-buhl)

(adj.) Something that is *obtainable* can be gained or attained by some action or effort.

6. achievable
(uh-CHEEV-uh-buhl)

(adj.) A goal that can be reached is *achievable*.

7. crust
(kruhst)

(n.) Earth's *crust* is the outer part of the planet.

(n.) The hardened outside surface or covering of something, such as bread, is the *crust*.

8. mantle
(MAN-tuhl)

(n.) The *mantle* is the part of the Earth found between the crust (the outer layer) and the core.

(n.) Anything that covers or envelops something the way a cape does can be called a *mantle*.

9. alter
(AWL-tur)

(v.) When you *alter* something, you change it.

10. landscape
(LAND-skape)

(n.) The *landscape* is the landforms in a particular area or region.

Each lesson word has been placed in a category. With a partner, discuss and list items that belong in each category. Compare your results with those of another pair of students.

Goals That Are *Achievable*

Objects That Cause Damage When They *Collide* with Something

Elements of a *Landscape*

Things That You Can *Alter*

Results That Are *Obtainable*

Things Found on or in the Earth's *Crust*

Things Found Between Two Layers, Like Earth's *Mantle*

When You Might Experience a *Jolt*

Rules That Are *Invariable*

Signals of Danger

Check for Understanding

Choose the lesson word that completes each sentence. Write the word on the line provided. Some words will be used twice.

> achievable   crust   mantle
>
> alter   invariable   obtainable
>
> collide   jolt   signal
>
> landscape

1. The Earth's core is completely covered by the _____.

2. The rules are _____, and you can't change them.

3. Free admission makes the concert a/an _____ event for anyone.

4. An earthquake can cause cracks and fissures in the Earth's _____.

5. After winning ten straight games, the team thought the championship might be a/an _____ goal.

6. Heavy snow and slippery roads caused many vehicles to _____.

7. Lightning is the _____ that thunder will soon follow.

8. The tremendous _____ from the explosion rocked the building.

9. The gale force winds uprooted trees and changed the _____ forever.

10. The snowstorm closed airports and forced thousands to _____ their travel plans.

11. People who don't look where they're going often _____ with objects.

12. To keep order, the talent show organizer announced that the order of the performances was _____ and he would not switch people around.

Expand Word Meanings

Read the paragraph below to learn other meanings for some of the lesson words.

The sounds of snowplows jolt me awake. Could these sounds signal a snow day? I slide under the warm covers toward the window, and without leaving my bed, I reach over, lift the shade, and peer out. It's still dark outside, and it's snowing. Our street is already blanketed with a thick mantle of snow. Bushes and cars are shapeless lumps beneath it. In the light of the streetlamp, the snow's crust sparkles like scattered diamonds. I switch on the radio and snuggle back in bed to wait for the announcement that our school is closed.

> ! Notice that the lesson's words are used in a different way here. Look at *mantle*. Here it means anything that covers something like a cape. Look at the other highlighted words. Can you figure out the meanings of the words as they are used here? Refer to page 72 to confirm meanings.

Apply Other Meanings

Complete each sentence with a highlighted word from the paragraph above.

1. A _____ that was like rubbery skin formed on the pudding that had been left uncovered.

2. If the groundhog does not see its shadow, it may _____ an early spring.

3. Hitting a pothole can _____ a car so badly that it knocks the wheels out of alignment.

4. My little brother likes to have the _____ cut off his sandwiches.

5. To keep her shoulders warm, the elderly woman wore a _____ that she had bought from Spain in 1939.

6. The flashing amber lights on the school bus _____ that the bus is getting ready to stop.

7. If you _____ the table, the water will spill out of the glasses.

8. The freshly baked pie had a flaky _____ that fell away from the filling when I stuck a fork in my piece.

9. Sneezing can sometimes _____ the beginning of a cold.

10. Everything in the untidy room was covered with a thick _____ of dust.

Word Associations

Use what you know about the lesson word in italics to answer each question. Circle the letter next to the phrase that best answers the question. Be prepared to explain your answers.

1. Which of these things is NOT *obtainable* by working hard?

   a. success in a job
   b. good luck
   c. the respect of others

2. Which is a *signal* that a thunderstorm is about to happen?

   a. birds flying south
   b. a brilliant sunset
   c. dark clouds in the sky

3. What is part of the Earth's *crust*?

   a. rocks and soil
   b. molten lava
   c. clouds and vapors

4. Which holiday is celebrated on a date that is *invariable*?

   a. Memorial Day
   b. the Fourth of July
   c. Thanksgiving

5. If you lost control while skiing, with what would you prefer to *collide*?

   a. a tree
   b. another skier
   c. a bank of soft snow

6. Which new thing is least likely to *alter* a person's appearance?

   a. a new idea
   b. a hairstyle
   c. a pair of glasses

7. Which event would have the least permanent impact on the *landscape*?

   a. an earthquake
   b. a rainstorm
   c. a tornado

8. Where is the *crust* on food?

   a. in the middle
   b. on the inside
   c. on the outside

9. Which of these seems like the most *achievable* goal?

   a. becoming an Olympic athlete
   b. getting a good grade in math
   c. winning a trip to a theme park

10. Which might give you a *jolt*?

    a. a funny joke
    b. a bump in the road
    c. a favorite song

Check Again

Use what you know about the lesson word in italics to complete each sentence. Be sure your sentences make sense.

1. If we *alter* our plans now, _____
_____

2. You might *collide* with other skaters if _____

3. The Earth's *crust* is similar to _____

4. One *invariable* rule at our house is _____
_____

5. We all felt a *jolt* when _____

6. The desert *landscape* was graced by _____

7. Something that is like a *mantle* _____

8. My most *obtainable* goal for this year is _____
_____

9. A raised hand is often the *signal* that _____

10. This may not be *achievable,* but someday I want _____
_____

Challenge Yourself

Follow the directions to write sentences with the lesson words in italics. Be sure your sentences make sense both grammatically and in meaning.

1. Write a sentence with the word *collide* in the seventh position.

2. Write a sentence exactly nine words in length using the word *landscape*.

3. Write a sentence with the word *alter* in the fourth position.

Word-Solving Strategies:
Suffixes

The suffix –able: "able to"

Prefixes can be added to the beginnings of words. Suffixes can be added to the ends of words and change the words' parts of speech. For example, the suffix *-able* can be added to a verb to create an adjective.

Take the word *obtainable* from this lesson. The verb *obtain*—meaning "to gain or attain"—becomes the adjective *obtainable* when the suffix *-able* is added. The adjective means "able to be gained or attained." Something that is *obtainable* is something you can get by making an effort.

Analyze the word *achievable* from the lesson. The verb *achieve* means "to carry out successfully or accomplish." By adding the suffix *-able*, the verb becomes an adjective that means "able to be carried out successfully or able to be accomplished." Note that the final *e* in *achieve* is dropped when the suffix

is added. The final *e* is always dropped when *-able* is added to a verb except when a verb ends with *ce* or *ge*. When *-able* is added to *replace*, for example, the final *e* is not dropped. The adjective is spelled *replaceable*.

Examples

Study these examples of verbs that are changed to adjectives by adding *-able*. Note when the final *e* in the verb is dropped when the suffix is added and when it is not.

search → searchable
move → movable
notice → noticeable
teach → teachable
know → knowable
walk → walkable

BE CAREFUL!

There are words that end with *-ible* instead of *-able*. When a verb ends with *ss*, the suffix is spelled *-ible*: *dismiss, dismissible; express, expressible.* But most words that end with *-ible* are formed by adding the suffix to a word part rather than a whole word. Examples of this are *permissible, incredible,* and *terrible.*

Practice

Use what you've learned about the suffix *–able* to create adjectives from the following verbs.

1. approach _____

2. describe _____

3. afford _____

4. recharge _____

5. understand _____

6. debate _____

7. manage _____

8. profit _____

9. believe _____

10. reach _____

Practice for Tests

Fill in the bubble next to the answer that best completes the sentence or answers the question.

1. Read this sentence.

   When Mount St. Helens erupted in 1980, it dramatically changed the *landscape*.

   Landscape means:
   - **A** the landforms in an area
   - **B** the view from a particular spot
   - **C** a painting of an outdoor scene
   - **D** the attitude of a group of people

2. Objects *collide* when they:
   - **A** are painted different colors
   - **B** represent different ideas
   - **C** match perfectly
   - **D** crash into each other

3. Which of these is NOT a *mantle*?
   - **A** a blanket wrapped around you
   - **B** the icing on a cake
   - **C** the bubblegum in a lollipop
   - **D** a cape

4. A synonym for *alter* is:
   - **A** change
   - **B** stumble
   - **C** disagree
   - **D** permit

5. The opposite of *invariable* is:
   - **A** worthless
   - **B** permanent
   - **C** changeable
   - **D** same

6. Read this sentence:

   Unusual animal behavior can be a *signal* of a coming volcanic eruption.

   Signal means:
   - **A** consequence
   - **B** event
   - **C** measure of strength
   - **D** warning sign

7. Something that is *obtainable* can be:
   - **A** confined
   - **B** achieved
   - **C** persuaded
   - **D** seen clearly

8. When you feel a *jolt*, you might:
   - **A** react with a jump
   - **B** run for cover
   - **C** lose consciousness
   - **D** cheer and applaud

9. If the Earth's core is compared with the yolk of an egg, the *crust* is:
   - **A** the egg white
   - **B** a hardboiled egg
   - **C** the eggshell
   - **D** the egg yolk

10. A person who sets *achievable* goals:
    - **A** doesn't live up to expectations
    - **B** is not likely to be frustrated
    - **C** usually disappoints people
    - **D** has low expectations

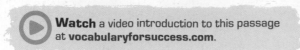 **Watch** a video introduction to this passage at **vocabularyforsuccess.com**.

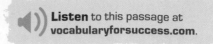 **Listen** to this passage at **vocabularyforsuccess.com**.

Hurricane Hunters

\<career profile\>

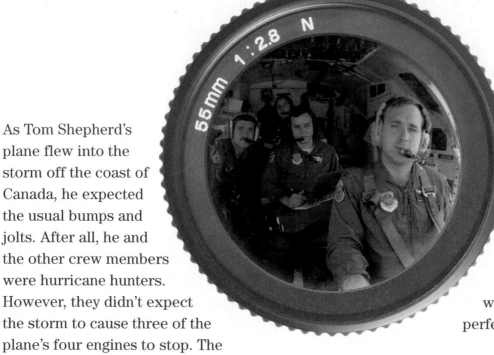

As Tom Shepherd's plane flew into the storm off the coast of Canada, he expected the usual bumps and jolts. After all, he and the other crew members were hurricane hunters. However, they didn't expect the storm to cause three of the plane's four engines to stop. The plane began to fall from the sky.

Why would hurricane hunters put themselves through such an ordeal? Despite the danger, hurricane hunters go on aerial missions because scientists on the ground can't get all the information they need to save lives. "It's not about the thrill and excitement of hurricanes," says Jim McFadden of the Aircraft Operations Center. "This is a really tough job."

A tropical climate is the source of most hurricanes. When air is warm, it will expand and rise to create clouds and rain. These are the seeds of a tropical storm. A storm will gather speed if its winds combine with water temperatures that are at least 80 degrees Fahrenheit. Evaporation, a part of the water cycle, gives the storm even more power. To be considered an actual hurricane, a storm must have wind speeds of at least 74 miles per hour. These winds must also spin in a perfectly closed circle.

What do hurricane hunters do on the job? They fly through strong winds into the eye of the hurricane, its calmest part. Then they drop instruments into the atmosphere to take measurements, such as wind speed and temperature. Hurricane forecasters on the ground study this information to determine the hurricane's path. Officials decide if people should leave their homes and go somewhere safe. Hurricanes are dangerous, but evacuation can be a hardship for those who must go. Making the right decision is a challenge, but officials know that safety is most important.

Just as Shepherd's plane came close to falling into the ocean, a second engine suddenly restarted. The hurricane hunters were safe, and they could continue their important work.

TALK ABOUT IT

With a partner, answer the questions below. Use as many of the highlighted words in the selection as you can.

1. What do you think is the biggest *challenge* for a hurricane hunter? Why?

2. Why is it important for hurricane hunters to gather information from the *atmosphere*?

Left: Hurricane hunters in the cockpit of their plane as they search for a storm.

Below: A view of hurricane clouds from the inside of the plane.

LESSON 8

Word Meanings

vocabularyforsuccess.com

▶ **Watch** a video introduction for each word

◀) **Listen** to iWords

📕 **Refer** to the online dictionary

For each highlighted word on pages 80–81, the meaning is given below. For practice with other meanings, see pages 85–87. For synonyms and antonyms, see page 100.

1. ordeal
(or-DEEL)

(n.) An *ordeal* is a difficult or painful experience.

2. despite
(di-SPITE)

(prep.) If you do something *despite* being warned against it, you do it in spite of the warning.

3. aerial
(AIR-ee-uhl)

(adj.) When something is described as *aerial*, it is done in the air or from the air.

4. climate
(KLYE-mit)

(n.) *Climate* refers to the temperature, wind speed, rainfall, and other weather conditions in a given region over a long period of time. The *climate* in Brazil is warm and humid.

5. source
(sorss)

(n.) The *source* is the point of origin—where something comes from or begins.

(n.) Someone or something that provides information is also a *source*—for example, a dictionary is a *source* for word meanings.

6. expand
(ek-SPAND)

(v.) When things *expand,* they increase in size, volume, or number.

7. cycle
(SYE-kuhl)

(n.) A series of events that are repeated regularly and always lead back to the starting point is a *cycle*.

(v.) When people ride their bikes to school or work, they *cycle* to the places they need to go.

8. atmosphere
(AT-muhss-fihr)

(n.) The air that surrounds the Earth is the *atmosphere*.

(n.) The *atmosphere* of a place is the mood or feelings that exist there.

9. hardship
(HARD-ship)

(n.) A *hardship* is something that causes suffering or forces people to do without things they need or are used to having.

10. challenge
(CHAL-uhnj)

(n.) Something that is difficult and requires extra effort to achieve is a *challenge*.

(v.) When you *challenge* someone, you invite that person to compete with you in the sport, game, or some other kind of contest.

Word Talk

Each lesson word is listed here. With a partner, take turns drawing a picture to illustrate the meaning of six of the words. As one partner draws, the other partner identifies the vocabulary word.

aerial

atmosphere

challenge (n.)

climate

cycle (n.)

despite

expand

hardship

ordeal

source

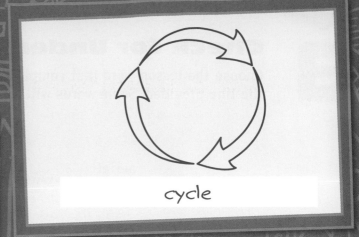

cycle

Check for Understanding

Choose the lesson word that completes each sentence. Write the word on the line provided. Some words will be used twice.

aerial	climate	hardship
atmosphere	cycle	ordeal
challenge	despite	source
	expand	

1. The wash _____ takes about a half-hour, because the machine has to wash, rinse, and spin the clothes.

2. Lake Itasca in northern Minnesota is the _____ of the Mississippi River.

3. In the winter, some people like to vacation in a warm _____.

4. The Earth's _____ is made up primarily of nitrogen and oxygen.

5. Since we depend on electricity, it's a/an _____ to go without it.

6. _____ photography provides a view of the ground from the sky.

7. The magazine started a campaign to _____ its readership.

8. Taking a vision test can be a/an _____ for people who are near-sighted.

9. Some dogs may not do well on obedience tests _____ being coached by their owners.

10. What one person considers a/an _____ might be easy for another.

11. Polar bears' bodies have adapted to the extreme cold of the Arctic Circle _____.

12. To _____ the size of the bubble, I blew the gum.

Expand Word Meanings

Read the paragraph below to learn other meanings for some of the lesson words.

The atmosphere in the bike store was hectic. Jasmine had asked Linda to come with her to buy a new bike and to keep her focused. When the bike clerk started pressuring Jasmine to buy a very expensive bike, Jasmine stood her ground. "My bike source said he can cycle fine on the cheaper model," she explained. Linda nodded in agreement and added that the clerk should not challenge Jasmine's decision. Finally the salesman brought the cheaper bike forward so Jasmine could hop on. Boy, was Jasmine glad she brought Linda with her for back-up!

> Notice that the lesson's words are used is a different way here. For example, look at *cycle*. Here it's a verb for riding a bike. Look at the highlighted words and try to figure out what they mean as they are used here. You can refer to page 82 to check if the meanings you thought of are correct.

Apply Other Meanings

Complete each sentence with a highlighted word from the paragraph above.

1. A comic book is usually a poor _____ for reliable facts and realistic story lines.

2. The _____ backstage before the play began was full of tension and nervous energy.

3. An encyclopedia is always a good _____ of basic information on a topic.

4. You can improve your chess skills if you _____ better players to play against you.

5. Fifty-five percent of the people in Copenhagen _____ to work every day.

6. Good teachers create a/an _____ that encourages learning in their classrooms.

7. Many people like to _____ for exercise and recreation.

8. Even though the _____ in the room seemed slightly angry, the speaker was able to persuade the audience to understand his point of view.

9. Our school will _____ other regional schools in a volleyball tournament.

10. A parent can be a useful _____ of good advice.

Word Associations

finish line

Use what you know about the lesson word in italics to answer each question. Circle the letter next to the phrase that best answers the question. Be prepared to explain your answers.

1. Which would NOT be found in a tropical *climate*?

   a. a rainforest

   b. a desert

   c. an iceberg

2. What transportation is crucial for *aerial* photography?

   a. a plane

   b. a boat

   c. a train

3. Which of these electronics is NOT a *source* for music?

   a. radio

   b. global positioning system

   c. MP3 player

4. Which would you consider a *hardship*?

   a. having no homework

   b. having a party

   c. having no phone

5. Which vehicle do you ride when you *cycle*?

   a. motorcycle

   b. bicycle

   c. car

6. From which of these things does the *atmosphere* protect the Earth?

   a. alien invasions

   b. meteor showers

   c. ultraviolet solar radiation

7. Which experience could be described as an *ordeal*?

   a. a bicycle trip in the country

   b. getting lost in the woods

   c. a picnic at the beach

8. Which household item can *expand*?

   a. a sink

   b. a soup pot

   c. an air mattress

9. Which job requires commitment *despite* the danger involved?

   a. ballerina

   b. firefighter

   c. chef

10. What quality is most needed for someone who accepts a *challenge*?

    a. a desire to succeed

    b. creativity

    c. loyalty

Check Again

Use what you know about the lesson word in italics to complete each sentence. Be sure your sentences make sense.

1. *Aerial* photographs showed _____

2. The *atmosphere* surrounds Earth and _____

3. One *challenge* the world faces is _____

_____

4. The harshest *climate* for human survival is _____

5. A caterpillar ends its life *cycle* as a _____

6. The orchestra concert was a success *despite* _____

_____

7. Our school club decided to *expand* its membership by _____

_____

8. The worst *hardship* I can imagine is _____

_____

9. A pleasure trip can become an *ordeal* if _____

_____

10. The *source* of a river is _____

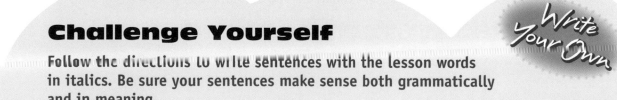

Challenge Yourself

Follow the directions to write sentences with the lesson words in italics. Be sure your sentences make sense both grammatically and in meaning.

1. Write a sentence with the word *ordeal* in the sixth position.

2. Write a sentence exactly seven words long using the word *atmosphere*.

3. Write a sentence with the word *despite* in the first position.

LESSON

Word-Solving Strategies: Context Clues

Contrast/Antonyms

Sometimes authors create contrasts in their writing that help you understand the meaning of an unfamiliar word.

> Despite the danger, hurricane hunters go on aerial missions because scientists on the ground can't get the information they need to save lives.

If you didn't know the meaning of *aerial*, the structure of the sentence would help you figure out that *aerial* must mean the opposite of "on the ground."

BE CAREFUL!

The word *not* or some other negative is often a signal for a contrast, but the contrast doesn't always involve antonyms.

It's the importance of the job, not the thrill, that inspires hurricane hunters.

There is contrast in this sentence, but *importance* and *thrill* are not antonyms.

Practice

A. Write a highlighted word and its meaning in the first two boxes. Then identify the contrast clue that helped you determine the meaning.

> When a destructive disaster such as a hurricane or earthquake strikes, there is no time for deliberation. First responders must make decisions quickly in order to help the most people. The same is true for medical teams, who need to act fast to ensure the greatest number of survivors. They prioritize the injured based on need. They don't try to treat everyone at once. Those whose conditions are the most precarious are attended to before those with more survivable injuries.

WORD	MEANING	CONTRAST CLUE

B. Write a sentence for each of the highlighted words from the paragraph above. Include contrast/antonym context clues.

1. _____

2. _____

3. _____

4. _____

88

Practice for Tests

Fill in the bubble next to the answer that best completes the sentence or answers the question.

1. Read this sentence:

   Traveling in an underdeveloped country can be an *ordeal*.

   Ordeal means:
   - ○ **A** adventure
   - ○ **B** difficult experience
   - ○ **C** learning experience
   - ○ **D** exploration

2. A word closely associated with *cycle* is:
   - ○ **A** pattern
   - ○ **B** mistake
   - ○ **C** activity
   - ○ **D** zigzag

3. The opposite of *expand* is:
   - ○ **A** withdraw
   - ○ **B** complement
   - ○ **C** elaborate
   - ○ **D** contract

4. Which circus performance is an *aerial* act?
   - ○ **A** trapeze artist
   - ○ **B** juggler
   - ○ **C** lion tamer
   - ○ **D** acrobat

5. If an assignment is a *challenge*, it is:
   - ○ **A** not graded
   - ○ **B** easily done
   - ○ **C** difficult
   - ○ **D** annoying

6. Read this sentence.

   Despite the disappointing weather, our fall festival was a success.

   Despite means:
   - ○ **A** in spite of
   - ○ **B** because of
   - ○ **C** as a result of
   - ○ **D** prevented by

7. A word closely connected with *climate* is:
   - ○ **A** mood
   - ○ **B** weather
   - ○ **C** planet
   - ○ **D** viewpoint

8. The *source* of something is its:
   - ○ **A** origin
   - ○ **B** effect
   - ○ **C** outcome
   - ○ **D** conclusion

9. In which group are all the items part of the *atmosphere*?
   - ○ **A** oxygen, water vapor, vitamins
   - ○ **B** oxygen, minerals, protein
   - ○ **C** oxygen, nitrogen, water vapor
   - ○ **D** oxygen, UV rays, color

10. People suffer *hardship* when they:
    - ○ **A** accept a challenge
    - ○ **B** lack necessary things
    - ○ **C** work too much
    - ○ **D** don't get enough sleep

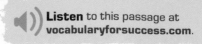 **Watch** a video introduction to this passage at **vocabularyforsuccess.com**.

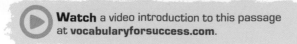 **Listen** to this passage at **vocabularyforsuccess.com**.

The Great Flood

<photo essay>

The worst flood in U.S. history took place in the spring and summer of 1993. For five months, there was so much rain that the Mississippi and Missouri Rivers were incapable of holding all of the water. The rivers overflowed and caused mass flooding in nine states. A natural disaster like this is generally thought to occur every 100 to 500 years. This one was called "The Great Flood of 1993."

Levees line many parts of the Mississippi and Missouri Rivers. Usually made of rock and soil, they're built to protect the land and people who live along the rivers. They keep the water from spilling into nearby towns. However, in this case, the constant rainfall was too much for the levees. On June 7, water went over the levees, breaking the barrier between the water and the land.

In the end, 80 percent of the levees failed to hold back the water. The result was that 75 towns were fully underwater. Damaged roads and highways made many areas completely inaccessible. For two months, no barges traveled on either river. Ten airports shut down, and railroads could not run. With no other means of transportation, people had to tour the damaged areas in a motorboat or other type of vessel.

The deluge killed 50 people and cost $20 billion. The water destroyed 20 million acres of crops. Erosion caused sand from the rivers to flow into nearby farmland and made that land unusable. Smaller debris, such as garbage, floated on the rivers alongside uprooted trees, bridge parts, and lumber. The roaring rivers were even able to buoy entire houses.

Could people have avoided the damage that the flood brought? Should the government have built better levees, or are homeowners, farmers, and businesses responsible for the risk they take when they live and work in a flood plain? Local, state, and national leaders know that when it comes to natural disasters and keeping people safe, there are no easy answers—but plenty of tough decisions.

Left: This house was underwater as a result of the 1993 flooding of the Mississippi River.

Below: During the same flood, a Coast Guard boat surveyed a downtown area.

VOCABULARY

incapable	deluge
mass	erosion
barrier	debris
inaccessible	buoy
vessel	risk

TALK ABOUT IT

With a partner, answer the questions below. Use as many of the highlighted words in the selection as you can.

1. Do you think that people are *incapable* of fighting the forces of nature? Explain.

2. What level of *risk* would you be willing to take to live where you wanted to live?

vocabularyforsuccess.com

▶ **Watch** a video introduction for each word

◀) **Listen** to iWords

Refer to the online dictionary

Word Meanings

For each highlighted word on pages 90–91, the meaning is given below. For practice with other meanings, see pages 95–97. For synonyms and antonyms, see page 100.

1. incapable
(in-KAY-puh-buhl)

(adj.) If someone is *incapable* of doing something, he or she lacks the necessary skill or capacity.

2. mass
(mass)

(adj.) A natural disaster that causes *mass* destruction affects a large number of people.

(n.) A *mass* is a large amount of something. The *mass* of an object is a scientific term that refers to how much material an object has.

3. barrier
(BA-ree-ur)

(n.) A *barrier* is a natural formation or a constructed fence or wall that stops the movement of something, such as water or traffic.

(n.) When people speak different languages, there is a language *barrier* that blocks communication.

4. inaccessible
(in-ak-SESS-uh-buhl)

(adj.) Something that is *inaccessible* cannot be obtained or is out of reach.

5. vessel
(VESS-uhl)

(n.) Any relatively large watercraft can be called a *vessel*.

(n.) Any container that holds something is a *vessel*.

6. deluge
(DEL-yooj)

(n.) A heavy rain—especially one that causes flooding—is a *deluge*.

(v.) If people *deluge* you with birthday cards, they give you lots of them.

7. erosion
(i-ROH-zhuhn)

(n.) When something is gradually worn away by wind or water, the process is called *erosion*.

8. debris
(duh-BREE)

(n.) The remains of something broken or destroyed are called *debris*.

9. buoy
(boy)

(v.) Something that lifts something else, such as an emotion or an object in water, is said to *buoy* it.

(n.) A floating object used to mark a boundary or underwater hazard is called a *buoy*.

10. risk
(risk)

(n.) A *risk* is the possibility of injury, loss, or danger.

(v.) If you *risk* breaking your leg, you do something that could possibly cause you to break your leg.

Word Talk

Each lesson word has been placed in a category. With a partner, discuss and list items that belong in each category. Compare your results with those of another pair of students.

Things Humans Are *Incapable* of Doing

Things That Are *Barriers*

Things That Are Affected by *Erosion*

Problems Caused by a *Deluge*

Seagoing *Vessels*

Things That Might Be *Inaccessible*

Places Where You Might Find *Debris*

Events That Cause *Mass* Destruction

Things That Can Be *Buoyed*

***Risks* That Are Reasonable**

Check for Understanding

Choose the lesson word that completes each sentence. Write the word on the line provided. Some words will be used twice.

barrier	deluge	mass
buoy	erosion	risk
debris	inaccessible	vessel
	incapable	

1. Beach grass protects sand dunes from _____.

2. A sudden _____ left big puddles of water on the soccer field.

3. In the 1930s, a radio show about alien invaders caused _____ panic.

4. Childproofing a house involves putting dangerous things where they are _____ to toddlers.

5. The survivors sadly picked through the _____ of their destroyed homes.

6. A grassy strip formed a/an _____ between lanes on a divided highway.

7. The speaker was so nervous that he was _____ of remembering what he wanted to say.

8. Because the sailboat was small, the _____ could not sail on the open sea since the rough waves would make the trip too dangerous.

9. Studies indicate that traveling by car presents a greater _____ than traveling by plane.

10. If you relax, the water will _____ you and you will float.

11. The fence provided a/an _____ that kept the dogs from leaving the yard.

12. Sandy was happy for the _____ since she wouldn't have to mow the lawn until the ground dried a bit.

Expand Word Meanings

Read the paragraph below to learn other meanings for some of the lesson words.

Ellen's friends had already launched their kayaks and were waiting for her in the lake. Near them, an empty bottle bobbed up and down like a buoy. The glass vessel nearly destroyed the natural beauty of the clear water. Fear was the barrier that kept Ellen from joining the others. Could she risk embarrassing herself in front of people? When her friends began to deluge her with questions about why she was keeping them waiting, she bravely slipped her kayak into the stream and paddled. The boat's heavy mass made her feel safe.

> **!** The lesson's words are used in a different way in this paragraph. Look at *buoy*. Here it's a noun describing an object that floats in the water. Look at the other highlighted words. Can you figure out the new meanings of the words as they are used here? Refer to page 92 to confirm what you infer about word meaning.

Apply Other Meanings

Complete each sentence with a highlighted word from the paragraph above.

1. When the vet examined my dog's leg, she felt a _____ and suggested we let her perform surgery to remove the lump.

2. Age doesn't have to be a _____ to understanding between young and old.

3. If you don't begin a project early enough, you _____ not being able to finish on time.

4. When politicians make unpopular decisions, people _____ them with angry e-mails and phone calls.

5. There was a pump at the campground, but we didn't have a _____ we could use to carry the water back to our tent.

6. Chris can be so short-tempered that people often agree with him rather than _____ an argument.

7. When our friends are sick, we _____ them with get-well cards.

8. Our cousins' lives are very different, and at first that was a _____ to our spending time together and having fun.

9. A thermos bottle is a _____ that keeps cold liquids cold and hot liquids hot.

10. In the race, the swimmers had to swim out to the floating _____ and back.

Word Associations

Use what you know about the lesson word in italics to answer each question. Circle the letter next to the phrase that best answers the question. Be prepared to explain your answers.

1. Which would you be likely to find on a sailing *vessel*?

   a. seat belts
   b. life jackets
   c. airbags

2. What would you want to have if you were expecting a *deluge*?

   a. rubber boots and a raincoat
   b. a warm parka and gloves
   c. hiking boots and a backpack

3. Which is a newborn *incapable* of doing?

   a. drinking
   b. breathing
   c. walking

4. What might cause a sudden *mass* exit from a movie theater?

   a. a boring movie
   b. a fire alarm
   c. a ringing cell phone

5. Which weather event is most likely to turn houses into *debris*?

   a. a thunderstorm
   b. a blizzard
   c. a tornado

6. Which situation would cause *erosion*?

   a. water running over rock
   b. rocks sliding onto a highway
   c. a tree branch scratching on a window

7. What *barrier* could keep people from walking on the grass?

   a. a gravel path
   b. a warning sign
   c. a hedge

8. What would be *inaccessible* if you had no boat and couldn't swim?

   a. the opposite end of a dock
   b. an island in the middle of a river
   c. the way to the bridge

9. Where would you NOT find a *buoy*?

   a. in a pot of water
   b. in a swimming pool
   c. in a lake

10. Which activity involves the least *risk* of injury?

    a. hockey
    b. chess
    c. cycling

Check Again

Use what you know about the lesson word in italics to complete each sentence. Be sure your sentences make sense.

1. The *barrier* along the parade route _____

2. Water will *buoy* _____

3. The *debris* created by the hurricane _____
_____

4. In preparation for the predicted *deluge,* we _____
_____

5. *Erosion* along the shore was caused by _____

6. It's unrealistic to wish for something as *inaccessible* as _____
_____

7. Most small children are *incapable* of _____

8. People are stunned by *mass* destruction such as _____
_____

9. I would be willing to take a *risk* in order to _____
_____

10. One example of an ocean-going *vessel* is _____

Challenge Yourself

Follow the directions to write sentences with the lesson words in italics. Be sure your sentences make sense both grammatically and in meaning.

1. Write a sentence with the word *barrier* in the fifth position.

2. Write a sentence exactly eleven words long using the word *inaccessible*.

3. Write a sentence with the word *risk* in the second position.

Word-Solving Strategies:
Prefixes

The prefix in-: "not"

You've learned how a suffix, which is added to the end of a word, changes the word's part of speech. A suffix can also change a word's meaning. A prefix is added to the beginning of a word. Prefixes can help you figure out the meaning of a word.

When you add the prefix *in-* to a word, you create a new word that means the opposite. The adjective *incapable* from this lesson is an example. If you are *capable*, you have the power or ability to do something. If you are *incapable*, you don't have the power or ability to do something.

The same is true for another lesson word, *inaccessible. Accessible* means "within reach." *Inaccessible* means the opposite: "out of reach."

When the prefix *in-* is added to an adjective that begins with *p*, the spelling of the prefix changes to *im-*. An example of this is *polite* and *impolite*.

The prefix *in-* can also be added to nouns. For example, *ability* means "skill." *Inability* means "lack of skill."

Examples

Read these words and think about how the addition of *in-* changes the meaning.

variable → invariable
experience → inexperience
comparable → incomparable
attentive → inattentive
convenient → inconvenient
sufficient → insufficient
coherent → incoherent

The word *invaluable* has the prefix *in-*, but its meaning is not the opposite of *valuable*. If things or people are *invaluable,* it doesn't mean they are not valuable. It means that their value is so great that it cannot be calculated. *Invaluable* is a synonym for *priceless,* which similarly doesn't mean that there is no price but that the value is beyond any price.

BE CAREFUL!

Practice

Use what you've learned about the prefix *in–* to create words that mean the opposite of the given word.

1. effective _____

2. correct _____

3. equality _____

4. decent _____

5. patient _____

6. humane _____

7. dependent _____

8. considerate _____

9. active _____

10. possible _____

Practice for Tests

Fill in the bubble next to the answer that best completes the sentence or answers the question.

1. Read this sentence.

   Owning a yacht is an *inaccessible* luxury for most people.

   Inaccessible means:

   - ○ **A** undesirable
   - ○ **B** achievable
   - ○ **C** unattainable
   - ○ **D** extraordinary

2. A word closely related to *incapable* is:
   - ○ **A** disqualified
   - ○ **B** unattainable
   - ○ **C** unconvinced
   - ○ **D** unskilled

3. Which of these is NOT a *mass?*
   - ○ **A** swarm of bees
   - ○ **B** clump of dirt
   - ○ **C** large group of people
   - ○ **D** light

4. In which group can all the items be a *barrier?*
   - ○ **A** levee, river, dam
   - ○ **B** fence, hedge, path
   - ○ **C** roadblock, road, wall
   - ○ **D** fence, wall, levee

5. When you take a *risk,* you:
   - ○ **A** avoid danger
   - ○ **B** play it safe
   - ○ **C** might get injured
   - ○ **D** do as little as possible

6. Read this sentence.

   The picnic was canceled because they were forecasting a *deluge*.

   Deluge means:

   - ○ **A** windstorm
   - ○ **B** heavy rain
   - ○ **C** freezing rain
   - ○ **D** hailstorm

7. An element that can *buoy* is:
   - ○ **A** wind
   - ○ **B** earth
   - ○ **C** fire
   - ○ **D** water

8. You would NOT use the word *vessel* to describe:
   - ○ **A** a small paddleboat
   - ○ **B** a sailboat
   - ○ **C** a cruise ship
   - ○ **D** a container ship

9. When something suffers *erosion,* it:
   - ○ **A** changes color
   - ○ **B** develops mold
   - ○ **C** is worn away
   - ○ **D** becomes a liquid

10. Another word for *debris* is:
    - ○ **A** destruction
    - ○ **B** remains
    - ○ **C** shortfall
    - ○ **D** worn-out

Synonyms and Antonyms

In the following Word Bank, you will find synonyms and antonyms for some of the words in Lessons 7–9. (Remember: Some words have both synonyms and antonyms.) Study these words; then complete the exercises below.

unrealistic	increase	result	opening	shifting	assessment
downpour	constant	change	certainty	guide	problems

A. For each sentence, fill in the blank with a SYNONYM for the word in boldface.

1. The club will _____ its rules so that members who cannot make all of the meetings will not have to **alter** their schedules in order to attend them.

2. We need to **expand** our efforts to help feed the homeless because the number of people who live on the streets continues to _____ .

3. The hurricane produced a/an _____ of rain that lasted three days. The **deluge** flooded the entire town.

4. The price of school lunch was **invariable** this year, remaining at a/an _____ $3 per meal.

5. After all the **hardship** the farmers faced from a lack of rain, more _____ came in the form of a swarm of locusts.

B. For each sentence, fill in the blank with an ANTONYM for the word in boldface.

6. The army placed a barrier in front of any _____ that the rebels could use to enter the city.

7. Con Yee thought winning the singing competition was **obtainable** until she lost her voice and realized her dream was now _____.

8. My uncle didn't worry about the **risk** he took skydiving because he felt safe with the _____ of his high-quality equipment.

9. After the plumber found the **source** of the leak and plugged the hole, my siblings and I cleaned up the huge puddle of water that was the _____ of the problem.

10. Due to _____ weather patterns, the usual, **invariable** date of the county fair will be moved to the fall this year.

Word Study: Proverbs

A proverb is a saying that gives advice or illustrates a commonly known truth. For example, "Don't count your chickens before they hatch," is advising you not to plan what you will do with something before you have it. "You can't judge a book by its cover" means not to make assumptions about people based on how they look. Many words in Lessons 7–9 relate to proverbs. For example, when faced with a challenge (Lesson 8), think of the proverb, "Where there's a will, there's a way" to remind you that if you are determined, you will find a way to meet the challenge.

Practice

Read each sentence. Use context clues to figure out the meaning of each proverb in boldface. Then, write the letter of the definition for the proverb.

_____ 1. Jeremiah knew he had to **strike while the iron was hot** to get tickets for the concert.

_____ 2. When Ada asked her father why he paid someone to change the oil in his car when he could do it himself, he said, "**Time is money**."

_____ 3. Benny didn't believe he could face another hardship until he remembered that **when the going gets tough, the tough get going**.

_____ 4. Megan apologized, but her friend said, "Just **let bygones be bygones**."

_____ 5. When the team was impatient about their long training, the coach said, "**Rome was not built in a day**."

_____ 6. When several volunteers came to clean the park, we realized that **many hands make light work**.

a. forgive and forget past arguments

b. how long a person spends on an effort is valuable

c. go for an opportunity as quickly as possible

d. don't give up if the task is an important one

e. sharing makes the job quicker and easier

f. doing something well takes time

g. strong people work harder as the job gets harder

Apply

Work with a partner to find out the meaning of each proverb. (Use an online or print dictionary.) Then work together to write a sentence for each item.

1. Let sleeping dogs lie.

2. Practice what you preach.

3. Every rose has a thorn.

4. Haste makes waste.

5. Leave no stone unturned.

6. A man is as old as he feels.

7. Walls have ears.

8. You reap what you sow.

Vocabulary for Comprehension

Read the following passage, in which some of the words you have studied in Lessons 7–9 appear in boldface type. Then answer questions 1–6.

Ice Storm!

An ice storm is often less destructive than an earthquake, a hurricane, or a flood. But it still has the power to **alter** the **landscape** and cause **hardship** for many people. In December
5 2008 an ice storm struck eastern New York. Trees cracked under the heavy **mantle** of ice. They brought down utility lines and caused **mass** power outages. Thousands of people had to endure the **ordeal** of living without
10 electricity for as long as two weeks. Electricity is necessary for most heating systems to function. Many homes were without heat in the cold Northeast **climate**.

Trees often fell onto roadways and created a
15 **barrier** that kept repair crews from getting through. Many areas were **inaccessible** until the **debris** could be cleared away. The **invariable** grinding of
20 chainsaws was a constant sound as people faced the **challenge** of clearing roads and restoring normalcy.

People found ways to cope **despite** their dependence on electricity for just about
25 everything. They learned that they were not **incapable** of getting along without lights, TV, and computers. They also discovered that surviving such a great inconvenience was an **achievable** goal.

1. In sentence 2, **alter** means
   - ○ **A** destroy
   - ○ **B** flatten
   - ○ **C** change
   - ○ **D** fix

2. The best adjective to describe an **ordeal** (line 9) would be
   - ○ **A** exciting
   - ○ **B** difficult
   - ○ **C** deadly
   - ○ **D** sturdy

3. A **barrier** (line 15) forces you to
   - ○ **A** see in either direction
   - ○ **B** move forward
   - ○ **C** go
   - ○ **D** stop

4. A synonym for **invariable** (line 19) is
   - ○ **A** unchanging
   - ○ **B** unpleasant
   - ○ **C** annoying
   - ○ **D** deafening

5. Someone who is **incapable** (line 26)
   - ○ **A** has the needed abilities
   - ○ **B** works until a task is done
   - ○ **C** has problems coping
   - ○ **D** is successful

6. A person who does NOT set **achievable** goals (line 29) can be
   - ○ **A** satisfied
   - ○ **B** content
   - ○ **C** neglectful
   - ○ **D** frustrated

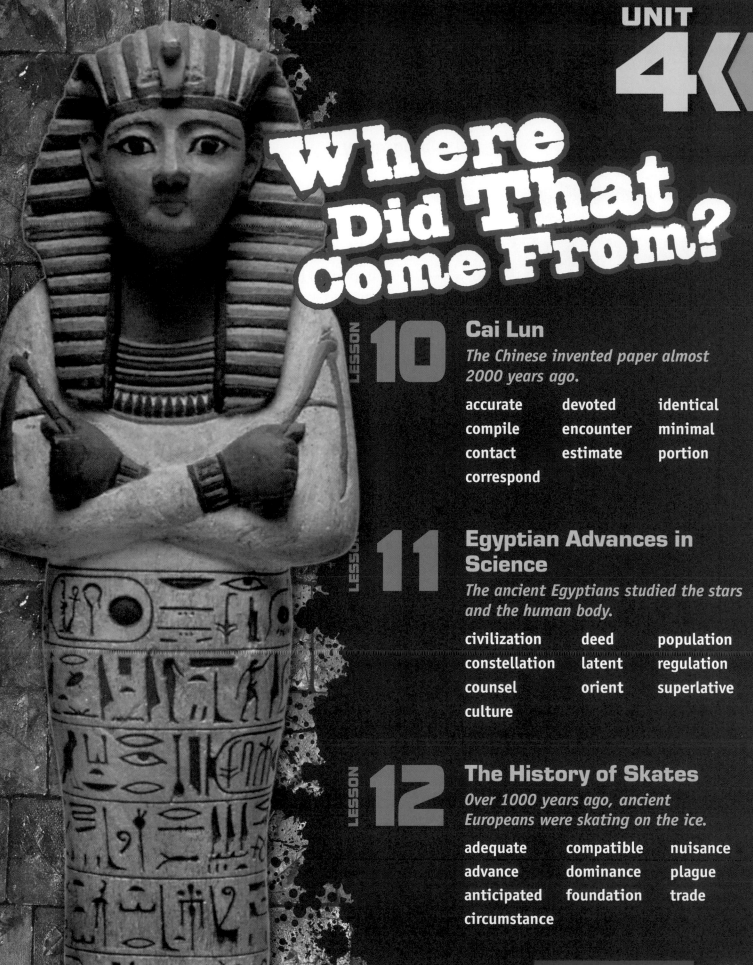

Where Did That Come From?

LESSON **10** **Cai Lun**

The Chinese invented paper almost 2000 years ago.

accurate	devoted	identical
compile	encounter	minimal
contact	estimate	portion
correspond		

LESSON **11** **Egyptian Advances in Science**

The ancient Egyptians studied the stars and the human body.

civilization	deed	population
constellation	latent	regulation
counsel	orient	superlative
culture		

LESSON **12** **The History of Skates**

Over 1000 years ago, ancient Europeans were skating on the ice.

adequate	compatible	nuisance
advance	dominance	plague
anticipated	foundation	trade
circumstance		

▶ **Watch** a video introduction to this passage at **vocabularyforsuccess.com**.

🔊 **Listen** to this passage at **vocabularyforsuccess.com**.

Cai Lun

<biography>

Paper—studies estimate that Americans use 85 tons of it each year. It's hard to imagine our lives without it. Luckily, we don't have to. That's because of the inventiveness, many believe, of a Chinese man who lived almost 2000 years ago.

Born in central China in 62 CE, Cai Lun supposedly joined the court of the Chinese emperor after completing his education. He was well-liked and was soon appointed the Emperor's Inspector of Weapons. That role led

to an encounter with the Dowager Empress Teng, who believed in Cai's potential. He then had to contact the Dowager Empress for the necessary finanacial backing, as well as her important political influence. The Empress's support may explain why Cai Lun devoted years to creating paper.

Before paper existed, people scratched symbols onto bones or drew on wet clay tablets. In Egypt, they wrote on slices of papyrus plant. In China and Japan, they painted on silk to correspond, or communicate in writing. Cai Lun created a new kind of writing surface. It was so light, strong, and easy to make that it changed the world.

How did Cai Lun make paper? He mixed old rags, fishing nets, and the bark portion of mulberry trees, bamboo, and other plant materials together with water. He pounded the mix into a wet pulp, placed it in molds, and let it dry. What remained was a thin layer of dense fiber—paper! It's accurate to say that

Cai Lun is thought by many to have been the first person to develop paper.

VOCABULARY

estimate	portion
encounter	accurate
contact	identical
devoted	compile
correspond	minimal

the process of making paper today, while not identical to Cai Lun's method, is very similar. Whether making paper by hand or on a huge machine, you still compile similar materials, mash them together, and let the liquids dry.

Although we know only a minimal amount about Cai Lun, we know he died in 121 CE. As Chinese paper-making methods spread around the world, so did reading and writing. Paper is considered one of the great inventions of the world. It's no wonder that many in China consider Cai Lun an important folk hero.

TALK ABOUT IT

With a partner, answer the questions below. Use as many of the highlighted words in the selection as you can.

1. *Compile* a list of the ways you use paper each day. Discuss as a class. Were the lists similar?

2. Is it *accurate* to say that in the future people won't need paper at all?

This method of making paper by hand has changed little since the time of Cai Lun.

vocabularyforsuccess.com

▶ **Watch** a video introduction for each word

◀)) **Listen** to iWords

📖 **Refer** to the online dictionary

Word Meanings

For each highlighted word on pages 104–105, the meaning is given below. For practice with other meanings, see pages 109–110. For synonyms and antonyms, see page 134.

1. estimate
v. (ESS-ti-mate)
n. (ESS-ti-mit)

(v.) When you *estimate*, you guess how much or how many.

(n.) An *estimate* is the amount or number that you guess.

2. encounter
(en-KOWN-tur)

(n.) A meeting of two groups or two people can be called an *encounter*. An *encounter* also takes place when a person comes upon an unexpected situation.

3. contact
(KON-takt)

(v.) When you *contact* someone, you meet or communicate with that person.

(n.) A *contact* is a person you know who you can talk with or write to for a specific reason.

4. devoted
(di-VOH-tid)

(v.) A person who is *devoted* to a project or cause spends a great deal of his or her time working on it.

5. correspond
(kor-uh-SPOND)

(v.) When you *correspond* with someone, you may write a letter or an e-mail to communicate with him or her.

(v.) When your ideas *correspond* with another person's ideas, you agree.

6. portion
(POR-shuhn)

(n.) A *portion* is a part of a whole. When you have a *portion* of something, you do not have all of it.

(v.) When you *portion* something, you divide it into many parts to give to others.

7. accurate
(AK-yuh-rit)

(adj.) An *accurate* document has no factual errors or mistakes in it.

8. identical
(eye-DEN-ti-kuhl)

(adj.) When two things are *identical*, they are the same. *Identical* twins are hard to tell apart.

9. compile
(kuhm-PILE)

(v.) When you *compile* what you need for a project, you put or bring materials together.

10. minimal
(MIN-uh-muhl)

(adj.) When something is described as *minimal*, it means the least amount. If your practice time is *minimal*, you spend very little time practicing.

Word Talk

Each lesson word has been placed in a category. With a partner, discuss and list items that belong in each category. Compare your results with those of another pair of students.

Things That Are *Portions* of a Whole	Tips for *Accurate* Writing

People or Ideas You Are *Devoted* To	*Encounters* That Are Sudden	Things That Can Be *Estimated*	Kinds of People You Want to *Contact*

Reasons to *Correspond*	Things That Can Be *Compiled*	Items That Are of *Minimal* Use	Things That Appear to Be *Identical*

Check for Understanding

Choose the lesson word that completes each sentence. Write the word on the line provided. Some words will be used twice.

accurate	correspond	identical
compile	devoted	minimal
contact	encounter	portion
	estimate	

1. The editor checked each fact to make sure the article was _____.

2. My mother plans to _____ with her long-lost cousin.

3. I will _____ everyone about the meeting by sending an e-mail.

4. The speed skater is so _____ to his sport that he spends several hours on the ice every day.

5. It will be easier to _____ the number of people at the concert than to try getting an exact count.

6. These pictures have small differences, so they are not _____.

7. We will need an hour to _____ all the materials for our class project.

8. Our family had time to see just a/an _____ of the theme park.

9. The explorers' first _____ with Native Americans was tense, but it ended peacefully.

10. This muffin is tasteless because of the _____ amount of flavoring.

11. The birthday cake was so big that we ate only a/an _____ of it.

12. Choose Web sites carefully, as many sites do not have _____ information.

Expand Word Meanings

Read the paragraph below to learn other meanings for some of the lesson words.

The history teacher realized that the class project on ancient inventions was difficult for many students. He suggested that the class portion the big project into smaller sections and work on them in groups. He also suggested more than one contact that students could interview as part of their research. Some students had difficulty figuring out an exact age for the artifacts. The teacher said it was okay to provide an estimate instead. Some groups were pleased to discover that their ideas would often correspond. That made it easier and faster to work together.

The highlighted lesson words are used in a different way here. For example, the word *portion* is used as a verb. How is the meaning related to the noun form? Look at the other highlighted words. Can you determine how they are used and what they mean? Refer to page 106 to confirm the words' meanings.

Apply Other Meanings

Complete each sentence with a highlighted word from the paragraph above.

1. Our math teacher explained that for some problems a/an _____ is better than an exact number.

2. If your ideas do not _____ with another person's ideas, you need to discuss where the differences are.

3. My aunt was able to expertly _____ the cake so that everyone received the same size piece.

4. If you decide to use a/an _____ for information, make sure that person is an expert on the subject.

5. Each group's plan should _____ as closely as possible, so that the project works when all the pieces are put together.

6. The chef was careful to _____ the work so that each assistant had a task to do.

7. We need more than a/an _____ to determine exactly how much material to buy.

8. We discovered that our beliefs _____ in many areas.

9. I think I have a good _____ who will be able to answer all of our questions.

10. The art gallery's director was unable to get a/an _____ of how many people came to the exhibit.

Word Associations

Use what you know about the lesson word in italics to answer each question. Circle the letter next to the phrase that best answers the question. Be prepared to explain your answers.

1. Which text would likely be the most *accurate*?

   a. an Internet blog
   b. a textbook article
   c. a letter to a newspaper

2. Which document would be nearly *identical* to the original?

   a. classroom notes
   b. handwritten letter
   c. printout from a copier

3. Which is a reason to *contact* someone?

   a. to say hello
   b. to shake hands
   c. to write a letter

4. Which word describes a *portion*?

   a. whole
   b. piece
   c. total

5. Which would best be described as an *encounter*?

   a. Mai choosing an item at the store
   b. Kevin studying hard for a test
   c. Mai and Kevin meeting unexpectedly

6. Why might people become *devoted* to a charity?

   a. they donate their time
   b. they lose interest
   c. they want to help

7. Which of the following would you need to *compile* to cook dinner?

   a. ingredients
   b. oven
   c. grocery store

8. Which item would require *minimal* materials to make?

   a. a car
   b. a birdhouse
   c. a school

9. Which would you NOT use to *correspond* with someone?

   a. a pen
   b. a telephone
   c. a computer

10. Which group would you *estimate* rather than count?

    a. people at a football game
    b. students in a classroom
    c. people invited to a dinner party

Check Again

Use what you know about the lesson word in italics to complete each sentence. Be sure your sentences make sense.

1. An *encounter* between two different cultural groups may result in _____

_____

2. A good reason to *compile* materials for a project is to _____

_____

3. When your ideas *correspond* to someone else's ideas, you may feel _____

4. *Contact* everyone about the meeting to _____

_____

5. An *estimate* is all you need when _____

6. If your coat is *identical* to someone else's, you should _____

7. A business needs *accurate* financial records to _____

8. When tornado damage is reported as *minimal*, you know _____

_____

9. If you are *devoted* to a cause, you _____

10. If you *portion* a pie, you _____

_____

Challenge Yourself

Write Your Own

Follow the directions to write sentences with the lesson words in italics. Be sure your sentences make sense both grammatically and in meaning.

1. Write a sentence with the word *estimate* in the fourth position.

2. Write a sentence exactly ten words in length using the word *accurate*.

3. Write a question about animals with the word *identical* in the fifth position.

LESSON **10**

Word-Solving Strategies:
Context Clues

Definition/Explanation

When you read an unfamiliar word in a text, you may find that the author has provided a definition or explanation. Read this sentence from "Cai Lun."

> In China and Japan, they painted on silk to correspond, or communicate in writing.

The word *or* is a clue that the text is defining **correspond**. The phrase *communicate in writing* provides the meaning of **correspond**.

BE CAREFUL!

A definition or explanation may not always follow an unfamiliar word. Check the context near the word or elsewhere in the text. Also look for the word *or* as a clue to a definition: *The encounter, or meeting, was friendly.* **Read carefully, because** *or* **is also used in a series:** *He had a choice of a pen, pencil, or chalk.*

Practice

A. Write the highlighted word and its explanation in the first two boxes. Then use the context clues to write another meaning for the word.

> "A seismic event has occurred," Zhang Heng reported to the Emperor hesitantly. He had invented an earthquake-detector box in which copper balls rolled off the flat surface of the object when the earth shook. But he could never guess how the Emperor would respond. He was loath to announce his news.
>
> "You say there has been an earthquake? Well, I have felt nothing, and you are obviously reluctant to tell me this news, so I am assured—confident that you are wrong," the Emperor declared.

WORD	EXPLANATION	WORD MEANING

B. Write a sentence for each of the highlighted words from the paragraph above. Use a definition or explanation as a context clue. You will use one word twice.

1. _____

2. _____

3. _____

4. _____

112

Practice for Tests

Fill in the bubble next to the answer that best completes the sentence or answers the question.

1. Read this sentence.

   The witness gave an *accurate* description of the event.

   Accurate means:
   - **A** factual or correct
   - **B** wrong or inexact
   - **C** sincere
   - **D** lengthy

2. When you *estimate*, you do NOT:
   - **A** guess
   - **B** judge
   - **C** predict
   - **D** measure

3. The opposite of *identical* is:
   - **A** same
   - **B** equal
   - **C** different
   - **D** similar

4. The best *contact* for information about hurricanes would be:
   - **A** a scientist who studies weather
   - **B** a science teacher
   - **C** someone who lived through a hurricane
   - **D** a resident of a tropical region

5. A word closely associated with *portion* is:
   - **A** togetherness
   - **B** contribution
   - **C** part
   - **D** total

6. Read this sentence.

   Some people can succeed with *minimal* support.

   Minimal means:
   - **A** nonexistent
   - **B** adequate
   - **C** significant
   - **D** very little

7. You would most likely *compile* materials:
   - **A** to delay a project
   - **B** before a project
   - **C** to avoid a project
   - **D** after a project

8. Which pair contains a celebration and holiday that *correspond*?
   - **A** fireworks, July 4
   - **B** evergreen tree, Valentine's Day
   - **C** candles, Flag Day
   - **D** birthday cake, New Year's Day

9. An *encounter* of forces on opposite sides is often:
   - **A** friendly
   - **B** expected
   - **C** violent
   - **D** confusing

10. Teens are least likely to be *devoted* to:
    - **A** sports
    - **B** carpentry
    - **C** music
    - **D** their friends

▶ **Watch** a video introduction to this passage at **vocabularyforsuccess.com**.

◀)) **Listen** to this passage at **vocabularyforsuccess.com**.

Egyptian Advances in Science

<textbook entry>

The period between 5500 and 332 BCE was an extraordinary time in ancient Egypt. Advances in astronomy, anatomy, and architecture helped this powerful empire dominate the ancient world. Archaeologists continue to study Egyptian society and culture today. They hope to discover more latent information about this remarkable civilization.

Studying the Stars   Today, astronomers study the sun, moon, and stars, but in ancient Egypt priests performed that job. To them, the stars were extremely important. They believed the movement of the stars could predict events. For example, the location of a star in the sky might indicate when the Nile River was going to flood. Then priests would counsel the farmers whose crops would benefit from the water. Egyptians also believed that it was possible to identify gods in the sky. Many historians suggest that the Egyptians linked Osiris, the god of death and rebirth, to the constellation known as Orion. Egyptians also used the stars in another way. They used them to help orient their buildings. This explains how the four sides of the pyramids always lined up north, south, east, and west.

Mummies: An Anatomy Lesson
Egyptians preserved the bodies of the dead because they believed that the bodies would be needed in the afterlife. Embalmers carried out this deed. They removed the organs and packed the body with a drying agent. Then they wrapped it in linen. This is one way the Egyptians came to know human anatomy.

People still marvel at the pyramids and wonder how they were built.

VOCABULARY

culture	orient
latent	deed
civilization	population
counsel	superlative
constellation	regulation

Architectural Marvels Egyptians began construction of the first pyramid in 2611 BCE. Approximately one hundred more were built. These enormous tombs housed the mummies of rich and powerful rulers, the most important members of the Egyptian population. It took thousands of people many decades to build these superlative stone structures. In 332 CE, Alexander the Great conquered Egypt. The result was that Egypt came under the rule and regulation of the Greek Empire.

This is one of the mummies that was found inside a pyramid.

This is an Egyptian map of the stars called a zodiac.

TALK ABOUT IT

With a partner, answer the questions below. Use as many of the highlighted words in the selection as you can.

1. What are two things you found interesting about ancient Egyptian *culture*? Explain.

2. How did the study of astronomy influence Egyptian *civilization*?

vocabularyforsuccess.com

▶ **Watch** a video introduction for each word

🔊 **Listen** to iWords 🎵

📘 **Refer** to the online dictionary

Word Meanings

For each highlighted word on pages 114–115, the meaning is given below. For practice with other meanings, see pages 119–121. For synonyms and antonyms, see page 134.

1. culture
(KUHL-chur)

(n.) A *culture* is a way of life—including values, ideas, beliefs, food, and art—shared by the same people.

(v.) A scientist will *culture* bacteria in nutrients to study their growth.

2. latent
(LAY-tent)

(adj.) A *latent* object or feeling is something that is hidden or out of sight until someone reveals it or makes it visible.

3. civilization
(si-vil-i-ZAY-shun)

(n.) A *civilization* is the characteristics of a culture—such as its literature, laws, technology, and political and religious organizations—that are identified with a certain group at a particular time in history.

4. counsel
(KOUN-suhl)

(v.) When you *counsel* someone, you advise or tell the person what to do.

(n.) A *counsel* may be a lawyer who advises people in legal matters.

5. constellation
(kon-stuh-LAY-shuhn)

(n.) A *constellation* is an arrangement of stars. The Ursa Major *constellation* has 16 stars arranged in the shape of a bear.

6. orient
(OR-ee-ent)

(v.) When you *orient* something, you set or locate it according to compass directions.

(n.) The *Orient* is an old word for the countries in Asia.

7. deed
(deed)

(n.) A *deed* is an action that you do or perform.

(n.) A paper *deed* is a document that shows you legally own a property.

8. population
(pop-yoo-LAY-shuhn)

(n.) The *population* of a place is the group of people or total number of people who live there.

9. superlative
(soo-PUR-luh-tiv)

(adj.) When an object or a performance is *superlative*, it is better than all others.

10. regulation
(reg-yoo-LAY-shuhn)

(n.) An organization that is under the *regulation* of another authority is operated according to that authority's rules and laws. A national park is under the *regulation* of the United States government.

Word Talk

Each lesson word is listed here. With a partner, take turns drawing a picture to illustrate the meaning of six of the words. As one partner draws, the other partner identifies the vocabulary word.

civilization

constellation

counsel (v.)

culture (n.)

deed

latent

orient (v.)

population

regulation

superlative

population

Check for Understanding

Choose the lesson word that completes each sentence. Write the word on the line provided. Some words will be used twice.

civilization	culture	population
constellation	deed	regulation
counsel	latent	superlative
	orient	

1. The senator performed a great _____ by fighting for that law.

2. Those pictures are _____, the best I have ever seen.

3. The lawyer planned to _____ the victims on what they could do to win their case in court.

4. The writing tablets showed that the ancient _____ was advanced.

5. The patient had a/an _____ condition that no one knew about until the doctor examined him.

6. Her _____ celebrates the holiday with traditional foods.

7. The _____ of Orion, or the Hunter, is visible on winter nights.

8. You did a good _____ by helping us with our food drive.

9. He asked which agency is responsible for the _____ of parades and other special events.

10. We will need someone to _____ us before we can file a complaint.

11. A compass will help you _____ yourself if you get lost in the woods.

12. Our town's _____ has grown quickly in the past few years.

118

Expand Word Meanings

Read the paragraph below to learn other meanings for some of the lesson words.

A wealthy man hired a lawyer as counsel to advise him on how to settle his grandfather's estate. Included in the paperwork was a deed saying the grandfather owned a valuable book about an Asian people who no longer existed. The title was *A View of the Lost Orient*. Unfortunately, the book was covered in a strange mold. The man was certain someone had purposely damaged it. He suggested that the lawyer have a scientist culture the mold to find out who. The lawyer laughed and said, "Only a wet basement is to blame for this now-worthless book."

> **!** Note that the lesson's words are used in a different way in this passage. For example, the word *culture* is used as a verb instead of a noun. Here it means "to grow something in a science lab." Can you figure out what the other highlighted words mean? Refer to page 116 to confirm meanings.

Apply Other Meanings

Complete each sentence with a highlighted word from the paragraph above.

1. A scientist has to _____ a virus sample carefully to make sure that nothing dangerous gets into the laboratory.

2. Long ago, when someone spoke of the _____, everyone knew that the topic was about the countries in the Far East.

3. A/An _____ is needed to show who the owners of the property are.

4. The medical team will need to _____ the infection before they know why so many people became sick.

5. In court today, the witness said she did not have to answer certain questions on the advice of her _____.

6. The _____ includes the countries of Japan and China.

7. An old _____ was found that proved the man actually owned the house.

8. The company will need an expert _____ to avoid legal trouble.

9. Part of our science lab project is to _____ some of the helpful kinds of bacteria.

10. The land will finally be ours when we sign the _____.

Word Associations

Use what you know about the lesson word in italics to answer each question. Circle the letter next to the phrase that best answers the question. Be prepared to explain your answers.

1. A *superlative* performance would be:

   a. boring
   b. wonderful
   c. good

2. Who could best *counsel* you on a matter related to your classes?

   a. doctor
   b. lawyer
   c. teacher

3. Which would have the largest *population*?

   a. city
   b. neighborhood
   c. village

4. An ancient *civilization* is marked by:

   a. electricity
   b. written records
   c. household appliances

5. When is the best time to see a *constellation*?

   a. dusk
   b. daytime
   c. nighttime

6. A good *deed* may be described as:

   a. a job finished on time
   b. something you feel good about
   c. an action that helps other people

7. If a group is under *regulation*, it is:

   a. ruled by another group or an agency
   b. prevented from operating
   c. limited in its membership

8. A good way to *orient* yourself if you are lost is to use:

   a. a ruler
   b. the position of the sun
   c. a weather vane

9. If you have a *latent* talent, you have:

   a. used it well
   b. not developed it
   c. shown it to only a few people

10. You can explore a *culture* by:

   a. learning how other people live
   b. researching what scientists do
   c. understanding weather patterns

Check Again

Use what you know about the lesson word in italics to complete each sentence. Be sure your sentences make sense.

1. The ancient Egyptian *civilization* is known for _____

_____

2. To help *orient* yourself when you are not sure you can find your way back from a place, _____

_____

3. A *deed* worthy of a hero might be _____

4. Cities need to know their *population* in order to _____

_____

5. You know that a game is *superlative* when _____

6. A *culture* may be recognized for _____

7. When looking at a *constellation*, it's fun to _____

_____

8. A *latent* illness is one that _____

9. It's important to seek *counsel* when _____

10. Professional sports teams are under the *regulation* of a governing association because _____

_____

Challenge Yourself

Follow the directions to write sentences with the lesson words in italics. Be sure your sentences make sense both grammatically and in meaning.

1. Write a sentence with the word *constellation* in the third position.

2. Write a sentence exactly eight words in length using the word *superlative*.

3. Write a question with the word *civilization* in the final position.

11 Word-Solving Strategies: Roots

The root **latus**: "carry," "bear," "bring"

Most English words are based on ancient Greek and Latin root words. You can use the meanings of these roots, along with what you know about prefixes and suffixes, to break down and figure out an unfamiliar word.

An example from this lesson is the word *superlative*. You have learned that it means "better than all others." If you didn't know the meaning of the word, you could use the prefix *super*, the Latin root *latus*, and the suffix *ive* to figure it out.

Break down *superlative* and see what happens. The prefix *super* means "above" or "beyond." The root *latus* means "carry," bear," or "bring." The suffix *ive* means "inclined to" and shows that the word is an adjective. So you could say that *superlative* describes something that is inclined to be carried above others—that is, *superior*, *better*. Remember

not to take all meanings literally when piecing together the elements of a word.

Another Example

Look at another example of using the root *latus* to determine the meaning of a word.

Word: *translate*

Breakdown: *trans* means "across"
                    latus means "bear"

Meaning: "to bring across"

If you check *translate* in a dictionary, you'll see that one meaning is "to remove or change from one place, state, or appearance to another." Notice how the word parts relate to the meaning of the whole word.

BE CAREFUL!

Some Latin and Greek roots have more than one meaning. For example, *latus* also means "wide," broad," or "side," as in *lateral* (extending from side to side). When using a root to figure out an unfamiliar word, check the context around the word to see if your word meaning makes sense.

Practice

Use what you've learned about the root *latus* to write sentences with the following words.

1. relate _____

_____

2. legislator _____

_____

3. collate _____

_____

4. elated _____

_____

5. translator _____

_____

6. dilate _____

_____

Practice for Tests

Fill in the bubble next to the answer that best completes the sentence or answers the question.

1. Read this sentence.

   My teacher hoped I would recognize and begin to use my *latent* talent for math.

   Latent means:

   ○ **A** hidden
   ○ **B** superb
   ○ **C** adequate
   ○ **D** creative

2. You would seek *counsel* when you:
   ○ **A** have finished your work
   ○ **B** have made plans
   ○ **C** know the answer
   ○ **D** need official help

3. A city's *population* is:
   ○ **A** children who attend school
   ○ **B** adults who are working
   ○ **C** all the people who live there
   ○ **D** all the people in apartments

4. Which of these is not a *civilization*?
   ○ **A** a musical group
   ○ **B** an ancient people
   ○ **C** a farming culture
   ○ **D** the Roman Empire

5. A word closely associated with *deed* is:
   ○ **A** thought
   ○ **B** hunger
   ○ **C** action
   ○ **D** stillness

6. Read this sentence.

   Many people celebrate their *culture* with special festivities.

   Culture means:

   ○ **A** growing bacteria in a lab
   ○ **B** a family name
   ○ **C** moving to a new home
   ○ **D** a way of life

7. A *constellation* is an arrangement of:
   ○ **A** pieces
   ○ **B** stars
   ○ **C** space
   ○ **D** animals

8. A *superlative* performance would be:
   ○ **A** impressive
   ○ **B** disappointing
   ○ **C** amusing
   ○ **D** terrible

9. A country under another nation's *regulation* is:
   ○ **A** independent
   ○ **B** oppressed
   ○ **C** controlled
   ○ **D** free

10. When you *orient* yourself, you find a:
    ○ **A** plan
    ○ **B** direction
    ○ **C** goal
    ○ **D** task

▶ **Watch** a video introduction to this passage at **vocabularyforsuccess.com**.

🔊 **Listen** to this passage at **vocabularyforsuccess.com**.

The History of Skates
<historical nonfiction>

Stand on a frozen pond or a skating rink and your first instinct is to glide. However, your feet alone aren't likely to be adequate for the task. The lack of friction on the ice will plague you. To advance forward without the nuisance of falling, you'll need some practice in addition to a pair of skates.

As is often the case with familiar objects, historians don't know who invented skates. Some believe the first skates appeared as long as 5,000 years ago! All agree, however, that 1,000 to 2,000 years ago, people in Finland and Holland were using skates.

Imagine this circumstance: long winters and frozen lakes and waterways. If you were going to market to trade or sell furs, it was faster to go across the water than around it. The piece of animal bone you laced to the bottom of your boot helped you move across the ice. That was the foundation for our skates today.

Over time, skates evolved from bone to wood to metal. Later, skates were combined with boots. For most people, skating was a means of transportation, not a sport. However, by 1642, Scotland had a skating club. While the English were introducing skating to the colonies one hundred years later, London was hosting a speed-skating race. In 1896, Russia held the first World Figure Skating Championships for men. Ten years later, women competed in Switzerland.

With the invention of refrigeration, the complete dominance of northern European skaters ended. In fact, Japan recently built an ice skating rink that is three acres in size. Today people can find skates that are compatible with any kind of skating activity—ice hockey, speed skating, or figure skating. The result is that the first skaters could not have anticipated how many people would owe them a debt of gratitude.

~VOCABULARY~

adequate	trade
plague	foundation
advance	dominance
nuisance	compatible
circumstance	anticipated

TALK ABOUT IT

With a partner, answer the questions below. Use as many of the highlighted words in the selection as you can.

1. Why would it be a *nuisance* to have to travel around a lake instead of across it?

2. Would you *trade* ice skates for a different kind of sports equipment? Why or why not?

Left: The earliest skates were made of bone and leather.

Above: A speed skater wearing special skates can move as fast as a car.

Word Meanings

vocabularyforsuccess.com

▶ **Watch** a video introduction for each word

◀)) **Listen** to iWords

📖 **Refer** to the online dictionary

For each highlighted word on pages 124–125, the meaning is given below. For practice with other meanings, see pages 129–131. For synonyms and antonyms, see page 134.

1. adequate
(AD-uh-kwit)

(adj.) When something is *adequate*, it is just sufficient or satisfactory.

2. plague
(playg)

(v.) A severe problem can worry, distress, burden, or *plague* you.

(n.) A *plague* is a terrible affliction, such as a deadly infectious disease.

3. advance
(ad-VANSS)

(v.) You can *advance*, or move forward, when your skills improve.

(n.) An *advance* is progress or a movement forward.

4. nuisance
(NOO-suhnss)

(n.) A *nuisance* is something or someone that is annoying or unpleasant. A buzzing mosquito can be a *nuisance*.

5. circumstance
(SUR-kuhm-stanss)

(n.) A *circumstance* is a special condition or fact that applies to particular events.

6. trade
(trade)

(v.) People *trade* when they exchange or purchase goods from others.

(n.) *Trade* is the business of buying and selling goods.

7. foundation
(foun-DAY-shuhn)

(n.) A *foundation* can be a base that provides support, such as the *foundation* of a house.

(n.) An organization supported by money for a special purpose is a *foundation*.

8. dominance
(DOM-uh-nuhnss)

(n.) To have *dominance* is to have control or success over all others.

9. compatible
(kuhm-PAT-uh-buhl)

(adj.) When two things or people are *compatible*, they fit or work well together and are in harmony.

10. anticipated
(an-TISS-i-pay-tid)

(v.) When you have *anticipated* something, you have looked forward to it or even predicted what would happen.

126

Word Talk

Each lesson word has been placed in a category. With a partner, discuss and list items that belong in each category. Compare your results with those of another pair of students.

Events That Are *Anticipated*	*Circumstances* for Which You Might Apologize

Things That Are a *Nuisance*	Signs That Friends Are *Compatible*	Things to *Trade* with Friends	Ways People Show *Dominance*

Foundations for Getting Good Grades	Things That Need to Be *Adequate*	Ways to *Advance* in a Job	Major Problems That *Plague* the World

LESSON 12

Check for Understanding

Choose the lesson word that completes each sentence. Write the word on the line provided. Some words will be used twice.

adequate	circumstance	nuisance
advance	compatible	plague
anticipated	dominance	trade
	foundation	

1. Progress on our project was _____ today, but there is still a lot more to do.

2. The team has proven their _____ by winning the championship.

3. The _____ of that building is very strong and sturdy.

4. She was able to _____ to the final round of the spelling bee by correctly spelling every word.

5. Choose someone you are _____ with in order to make the job easier and more pleasant.

6. I _____ that we would find this place because we had good directions.

7. According to the forecast, bad weather will continue to _____ us.

8. My grades are _____, but I want to improve them.

9. He was able to _____ seven baseball cards for the one card he wanted.

10. An unusual _____ caused me to be late for orchestra rehearsal.

11. Weeds in a garden are a/an _____ because they crowd other plants.

12. Please _____ me your apple for my pear.

Expand Word Meanings

Read the paragraph below to learn other meanings for some of the lesson words.

In the mid-1300s a plague spread through Europe, killing millions of people. The disease's advance caused whole villages to disappear as people died. Towns shut their gates and would not allow trade with outsiders. At that time in history, no one knew that poor sanitation, as well as the fleas carried by rats, helped spread the deadly disease. Today plague still exists all over the world, but it can be treated. A study in Colorado is looking at the role that climate plays in current outbreaks. The study is partly funded by the National Science Foundation.

> In this passage you can see that the lesson's words are used in a different way. For example, look at *plague*. Here it is used as a noun and refers to a deadly disease. Look at the other highlighted words. Can you figure out the meanings as they are used here? Refer to page 126 to confirm meanings.

Apply Other Meanings

Complete each sentence with a highlighted word from the paragraph above.

1. The parade's _____ was stopped when a cow wandered onto the route and wouldn't move.

2. A new _____ will support research into the causes of disease.

3. Bubonic _____ is carried by many kinds of rodents and can be deadly.

4. _____ along routes from Asia into Europe might have been one of the ways disease was spread long ago.

5. Without help from the charitable _____, we never could have raised funds to build the playground.

6. In many communities, outdoor markets are places where _____ is encouraged between residents and local merchants.

7. The development of the polio vaccine was an important medical _____.

8. The Internet has helped to spread a growing _____ in collectibles such as antique toys and crystal vases.

9. A/An _____ has been set up to collect money for disaster victims.

10. The most dangerous form of the _____ can cause death within a few days.

Word Associations

LESSON 12

Use what you know about the lesson word in italics to answer each question. Circle the letter next to the phrase that best answers the question. Be prepared to explain your answers.

1. Which event might be eagerly *anticipated* by students?

   a. a test
   b. an award ceremony
   c. detention

2. Which result shows *dominance*?

   a. a close race
   b. a tie score
   c. an easy victory

3. Which would NOT be a *foundation*?

   a. a high ceiling
   b. a wood floor
   c. a strong table

4. Under what *circumstance* might a school close for a day?

   a. opening of a new store
   b. a major snowstorm
   c. a local sports event

5. Which of these things would be the least *compatible*?

   a. computer and printer
   b. music and dance
   c. cat and mouse

6. Which phrase describes *adequate*?

   a. almost enough
   b. more than enough
   c. just enough

7. Which could be considered a fair *trade*?

   a. 4 quarters for a dollar
   b. 6 nickels for a quarter
   c. 9 dimes for a dollar

8. Which problem would most *plague* a farmer?

   a. cool days
   b. lack of rain
   c. a few weeds

9. Which would be the greatest *nuisance* at an outdoor picnic?

   a. a steady breeze
   b. flies
   c. some raindrops

10. Which of these might stop an *advance* of walkers?

    a. a roadblock
    b. a green light
    c. an escalator

130

Check Again

Use what you know about the lesson word in italics to complete each sentence. Be sure your sentences make sense.

1. A good *foundation* on which to set up a computer would be _____

2. A team is *compatible* when _____

3. To have *adequate* time to research and write an essay, _____

_____

4. A sports team can show *dominance* by _____

5. Something that could *plague* a person every day might be _____

_____

6. One way to stop the *advance* of an illness is _____

_____

7. Some people like to *trade* because _____

8. On a rainy day, a *nuisance* would be _____

9. A *circumstance* that would cause people to evacuate their homes would be _____

_____

10. An event that most students at this school have always *anticipated* is _____

_____

Challenge Yourself

Write Your Own

Follow the directions to write sentences with the lesson words in italics. Be sure your sentences make sense both grammatically and in meaning.

1. Write a sentence with the word *trade* in the third position.

Indians used trade a lot

2. Write a sentence exactly six words in length using the word *nuisance*.

That boy was loud, a nuisance

3. Write a question with the word *adequate* in the fourth position.

LESSON 12

Word-Solving Strategies: Suffixes

The suffix -ance: "state of," "quality of," "condition of"

When you see an unfamiliar word, you can break it into parts to help you understand what the word means. By looking at either the root of a word, a prefix added to the beginning, or a suffix added to the end, you can often define the word and figure out what part of speech it is.

When you see the suffix *-ance*, you will know that the word is a noun formed from a verb. The meaning of the suffix, which is "state of," "quality of," or "condition of," will give you a clue to the whole word's meaning.

An example of a lesson word with the suffix *-ance* is *dominance.* This noun is formed from the verb *dominate.* The suffix creates a noun that means the "state of" or "condition of" dominating or controlling.

Note that the spelling of many verbs does not change when the suffix *-ance* is added to form a noun. However, in some verbs, the final *-e* is deleted when the suffix *-ance* is added. In *dominate*, the *-ate* is dropped before adding *-ance.* When the spelling changes, you can still determine how the noun was formed, because the verb is still recognizable within the noun.

Examples

Look at these examples of verbs that have become nouns by adding the suffix *-ance.* Note that the spelling changes in some cases.

annoy → annoyance
grieve → grievance
hesitate → hesitance
repent → repentance
insure → insurance

BE CAREFUL!

Not all nouns that end with *-ance* are formed by adding the suffix to a verb. For example, the lesson word *nuisance* is a noun, but it is not formed from a verb. Use context to figure out the meanings of these words.

Practice

Use what you've learned about the suffix *-ance* to create nouns from the following verbs.

1. clear ______________________
2. avoid ______________________
3. tolerate ______________________
4. disturb ______________________
5. contrive ______________________
6. perform ______________________
7. guide ______________________
8. resist ______________________
9. accept ______________________
10. continue ______________________

Practice for Tests

Fill in the bubble next to the answer that best completes the sentence or answers the question.

1. Read this sentence.

   I thought my effort was *adequate,* considering how sick I had been.

   Adequate means:
   - ⚪ **A** satisfactory
   - ⚪ **B** outstanding
   - ⚪ **C** failing
   - ⚪ **D** useful

2. Something becomes a *nuisance* when it:
   - ⚪ **A** stops
   - ⚪ **B** helps
   - ⚪ **C** soothes
   - ⚪ **D** bothers

3. With which person or animal is a pet dog likely to be most *compatible*?
   - ⚪ **A** the mail carrier
   - ⚪ **B** a stranger
   - ⚪ **C** its owner
   - ⚪ **D** a squirrel

4. A disease becomes a *plague* when:
   - ⚪ **A** large numbers of people die
   - ⚪ **B** everyone gets sick
   - ⚪ **C** symptoms go away
   - ⚪ **D** it can be cured

5. Two people are *compatible* when they:
   - ⚪ **A** ignore each other
   - ⚪ **B** are assigned to work together
   - ⚪ **C** work well together
   - ⚪ **D** have many differences

6. Read this sentence.

   Taking algebra is a good *foundation* for learning more-advanced math.

   Foundation means:
   - ⚪ **A** follow-up
   - ⚪ **B** companion
   - ⚪ **C** solution
   - ⚪ **D** preparation

7. A soccer team will NOT *advance* if it:
   - ⚪ **A** beats the other team
   - ⚪ **B** loses to the other team
   - ⚪ **C** scores the most goals
   - ⚪ **D** has the best players

8. When you *trade* an item, you:
   - ⚪ **A** get something in return
   - ⚪ **B** prepare an item for sale
   - ⚪ **C** find a new use for the item
   - ⚪ **D** replace the item

9. A word associated with *dominance* is:
   - ⚪ **A** tolerance
   - ⚪ **B** special
   - ⚪ **C** strength
   - ⚪ **D** sufficient

10. Under what *circumstance* would a baseball game be canceled?
    - ⚪ **A** low attendance
    - ⚪ **B** heavy rain
    - ⚪ **C** team rivalry
    - ⚪ **D** injured player

Synonyms and Antonyms

In the following Word Bank, you will find synonyms and antonyms for some of the words in Lessons 10–12. (Remember: Some words have both synonyms and antonyms.) Study these words; then complete the exercises below.

guess	obvious	advise	insufficient	result	correct
withdraw	unclear	frozen	dedicated	pleasure	accomplished

A. For each sentence, fill in the blank with a SYNONYM for the word in boldface.

1. The scientist was sure her findings were **accurate** because she always took

_____ measurements to avoid making errors later.

2. The pep club **devoted** many hours to the project, which meant members

_____ most of their free time to getting it done.

3. My father would often **counsel** us to save our money, which is something I now

_____ my own children to do.

4. You can **estimate** the costs of caring for a puppy by trying to _____ how many cans of food he will eat in a week.

5. Jorge gave a **superlative** performance in the piano recital because he had become

quite _____ through extensive practice.

B. For each sentence, fill in the blank with an ANTONYM for the word in boldface.

6. The amount of food at the dance was **adequate** to feed all the attendees, but the

beverages were _____ so the organizers had to go buy more.

7. At first, the effects of the disease were **latent**, but they quickly became more

_____.

8. The pain and sweat that come with hard exercise are a **nuisance**. The _____ your body feels afterward, however, makes it all worthwhile.

9. The witness's descriptions were _____ , which made the police doubt that what he had told them was **accurate**.

10. During the battle, the general had to _____ his troops after severe losses. A few hours later he ordered them to **advance**, and they overran the enemy.

Word Study: Denotation and Connotation

Every word has a **denotation**, the literal meaning that you find in a dictionary. Many words also have a **connotation**, the feelings and images associated with a word. Connotations are usually described as being positive or negative. A neutral word has no connotations.

POSITIVE	NEGATIVE	NEUTRAL
sipped	gulped	drank
unique	bizarre	unusual
thrifty	miserly	economical

The word *encounter* in Lesson 10 has several synonyms: Think about the connotations of these words:

meet   **confront**   **greet**   **face**   **contact**

The words *meet, contact,* and *face* generally are neutral. However, *greet* has a positive connotation. It suggests two friends saying hello when they see each other. *Confront* has a negative connotation that suggests a hostile or angry encounter.

Practice

A. Circle the word in parentheses that has the connotation (positive, negative, or neutral) given at the beginning of the sentence.

neutral   **1.** The inventor (**gave**, **devoted**) his life to his work

positive   **2.** Your measurements for the banner are (**correct**, **exact**).

neutral   **3.** The two boys agreed to (**swap**, **trade**) their video game players for the weekend.

negative   **4.** The problems with my computer continue to (**plague**, **bother**) me.

positive   **5.** The witness needs some (**counsel**, **wisdom**) on how to answer the question.

negative   **6.** This idea for an automatic dog washer is (**clever**, **ridiculous**).

positive   **7.** The sounds coming from my sister's violin were (**musical**, **loud**).

B. Work with a partner. Write a plus sign (+) if the word has a positive connotation; write a minus sign (–) if the word has a negative connotation. Put a zero (0) if the word is neutral.

1. brillant ☐   **3.** contact ☐   **5.** thin ☐   **7.** nuisance ☐

2. interrupt ☐   **4.** scrawny ☐   **6.** portion ☐   **8.** superlative ☐

Vocabulary for Comprehension

Read the following passage, in which some of the words you have studied in Lessons 10–12 appear in boldface type. Then answer questions 1–6.

The Secret Cloth

Thousands of years ago, ancient Chinese **civilization** held a secret that was under the **regulation** of the authorities. Anyone caught revealing this secret was punished.

5 The secret was how silk was made. Silk is a **superlative** lightweight fabric that is warm in winter and cool in summer. It is made from the smooth, fine fiber of the silkworm cocoon. It takes 30,000 worms to produce just 12 pounds 10 of raw silk. Some people **estimate** that 3,000 cocoons are needed to make one yard of fabric.

Long ago, only royalty or wealthy people were allowed to wear silk. The Chinese even used the cloth as money. Their **dominance** of the

15 silk **trade** lasted for hundreds of years, until the secret left the **Orient** with immigrants and began to travel westward. India's **contact** with these immigrants led to silk production there.

In 550 CE, two monks appeared before Emperor 20 Justinian in Constantinople and told of an amazing **deed**. They had smuggled silkworm eggs inside their bamboo walking sticks. These tiny eggs became the **foundation** of a new silk industry. In the 1200s, silk weavers brought a 25 **portion** of the silk industry to Italy. By then, making silk was no longer a well-kept secret.

1. In sentence 1, **regulation** means:
   - A control
   - B threat
   - C idea
   - D topic

2. A **superlative** fabric (line 6) would be fabric that:
   - A rips easily
   - B is uncomfortable
   - C is inexpensive
   - D has many benefits

3. When you have **dominance** (line 14) over others, you:
   - A are responsible
   - B do all the work
   - C are in control
   - D are at the bottom

4. In the passage, **Orient** (line 16) refers to:
   - A a part of the world
   - B finding your direction
   - C the name of a company
   - D having to move away

5. The best **foundation** (line 23) for starting a new business would be:
   - A a beautiful building
   - B a display area
   - C a great product
   - D nice salespeople

6. A **portion** (line 25) is:
   - A a complete item
   - B fully visible
   - C a crack or break
   - D a section

Using Context

Circle the word that best completes each sentence. Note that the choices are related forms of the vocabulary words in the box.

assist	correspond	entrust
buoy	cultivate	estimate
collide	distribute	identical
compile	dominance	invariable
construct	embark	origin
control	enable	translate

1. We helped with the (**construction/cultivation**) of the doghouse by bringing all of the building materials.

2. The detective collected (**estimations/correspondence**) that showed that the suspect had written several letters to the victim.

3. (**Embarkation/Buoyancy**) is scheduled for early tomorrow morning, so everyone needs to be at the dock and ready to board the ship.

4. The king will be (**entrusting/enabling**) the messenger with the safe delivery of the package.

5. The company president asked her (**dominant/assistant**) to help set up the meeting.

6. Our team leader is the (**translator/originator**) of the idea for the social studies project.

7. Luckily, the (**collision/compilation**) was not serious, and the passengers in the two cars that hit each other walked away without any injuries.

8. Our family (**invariably/identically**) eats at the same restaurant Friday nights, so there is no reason to ask where we're going for dinner.

9. Hannah's job involved (**translating/distributing**) the article from French to English.

10. The workers do not like their current boss because he is so (**assisting/controlling**) and never lets them make decisions on their own.

Analogies

Read each sentence stem carefully. Then complete the sentence so that it makes sense. Use the relationship between the words in italics to help you.

1. A student who does *adequate* work will get average grades, while a student who does *superlative* work _____

   _____

2. Two people who have different points of view might have an *argument*, while two people who are *compatible* _____

   _____

3. Asthma will narrow a person's airways and *restrict* breathing, while an inhaler sends medicine to the lungs to *expand* _____

   _____

4. *Global* refers to the whole Earth, while a *hemisphere* _____
   _____

5. Someone with a positive attitude will feel that a goal is *achievable*, while someone who views himself or herself as *incapable* _____

   _____

6. A person who works in a *haphazard* way has no plan, while a person with an organized *approach* _____

   _____

7. The *transition* to a new school can be an *ordeal* for some students, while some students do well with the change because _____

   _____

8. A cat who has *devoted* itself to its owner often likes to stay nearby, while a cat who has not will go off by itself *despite* _____

   _____

Word Relationships

Read each question carefully. Think about the relationship between the two vocabulary words in italics. Then write an explanation that answers each question.

1. How is an *atlas invaluable* when you are studying the world?

_____

_____

_____

2. What might be a *circumstance* that causes *erosion* on a steep hill?

_____

_____

_____

3. What is an *issue* that would be interesting for a *debate*?

_____

_____

_____

4. What does a *barren landscape* look like?

_____

_____

_____

5. What should a *witness* do to be more *accurate* about what he or she saw?

_____

_____

_____

6. Why is it important for people to *reassess* a *bias* they might have about an issue?

_____

_____

_____

Generating Sentences

**Follow the directions to write sentences with the vocabulary words in italics.
Be sure your sentences make sense both grammatically and in meaning.**

1. Use the word *migrate* in a sentence about birds.

_____

_____

2. Use the word *document* in a sentence that is 10 words long.

_____

_____

3. Use the word *deluge* in the fifth position of a sentence of 15 words.

_____

_____

4. Use the word *hypothesis* in a sentence of exactly 14 words about sleep.

_____

_____

5. Use the word *explanation* in the second position of a question.

_____

_____

Extend Your Sentence

**Choose one of your sentences and turn it into a paragraph. Use at least four other
words from Units 1–4 in your paragraph.**

_____

_____

_____

_____

_____

_____

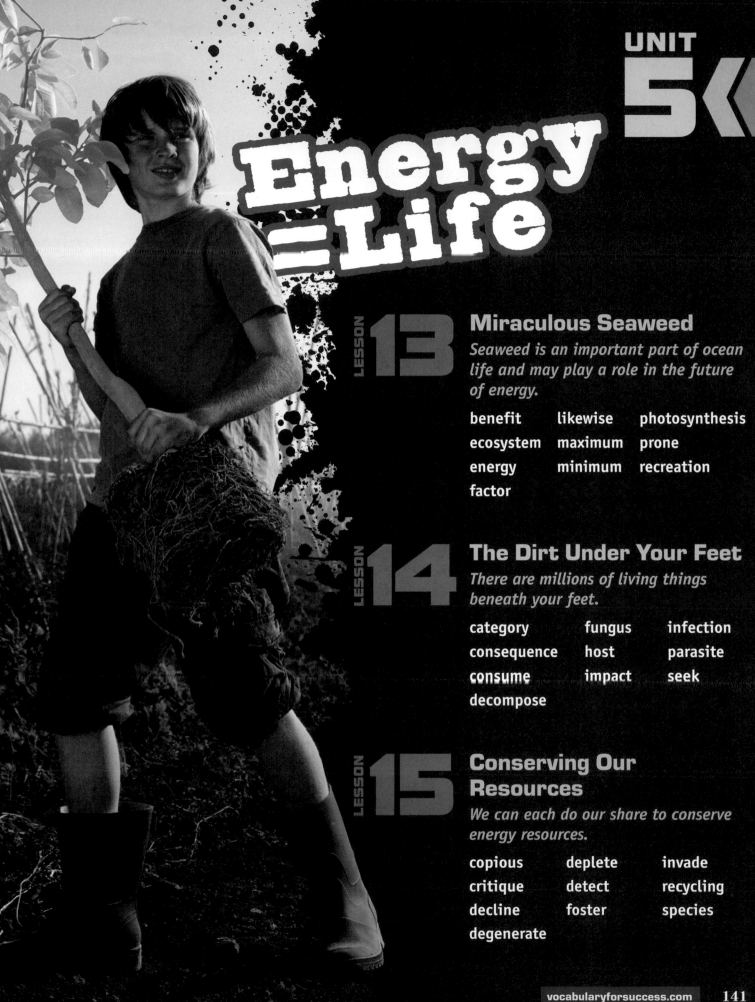

Energy =Life

LESSON **13**

Miraculous Seaweed

Seaweed is an important part of ocean life and may play a role in the future of energy.

benefit	likewise	photosynthesis
ecosystem	maximum	prone
energy	minimum	recreation
factor		

LESSON **14**

The Dirt Under Your Feet

There are millions of living things beneath your feet.

category	fungus	infection
consequence	host	parasite
consume	impact	seek
decompose		

LESSON **15**

Conserving Our Resources

We can each do our share to conserve energy resources.

copious	deplete	invade
critique	detect	recycling
decline	foster	species
degenerate		

▶ **Watch** a video introduction to this passage at **vocabularyforsuccess.com**.

🔊 **Listen** to this passage at **vocabularyforsuccess.com**.

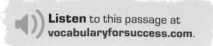

Miraculous Seaweed

\<expository essay\>

If you've walked for recreation near the ocean, you've likely seen seaweed on the shore. It can be delicate and feathery or hard and leathery, the size of a lettuce leaf or of a 20-foot hose. Scientists estimate that there are a minimum of 1,000 to a maximum of 10,000 kinds of seaweed. Although it is technically not a plant, seaweed looks and acts like one. Like plants, seaweed needs sunlight. Likewise, through photosynthesis, it uses sunlight to produce energy that other living things consume.

An ecosystem is a community of plants and animals that live together. Change any one part of the ecosystem and you risk changing the rest. Providing both oxygen and food for fish, seaweed is a key factor in an ocean ecosystem. It also provides places for fish to hide and to lay their eggs. A study of one seaweed bed off the Virginia coast revealed 8,200 fish in one square meter, while only 300 fish were outside of it. Imagine what would happen if no seaweed lived in the ocean!

Humans benefit from seaweed in many ways. It is used in medicines, soaps, sushi, soup, and even ice cream. Now some scientists believe they have found an extraordinary new use for seaweed. It can be turned into fuel to help meet the world's energy needs.

~ VOCABULARY ~

recreation	energy
minimum	ecosystem
maximum	factor
likewise	benefit
photosynthesis	prone

Today, seaweed is harvested from the ocean. In places like Japan and Bali, it's also grown in man-made ocean "farms." If both methods are used, the world may, in the future, have a never-ending supply of seaweed. However, ocean ecosystems are delicate and prone to damage. They rely on the proper balance of sunlight and plant and animal life. In our eagerness to get seaweed, it is important that we do not harm key ecosystems. If we can make sure that damage won't happen, look for fuels made from seaweed coming from an ocean farm near you.

Seaweed is wrapped around rice in sushi.

TALK ABOUT IT

With a partner, answer the questions below. Use as many of the highlighted words in the selection as you can.

1. What kinds of living things might you find in an ocean *ecosystem*? Make a list of as many as you can.

2. How would we *benefit* from using seaweed as an energy source?

13 Word Meanings

For each highlighted word on pages 142–143, the meaning
is given below. For practice with other meanings, see pages
147–149. For synonyms and antonyms, see page 172.

▶ **Watch** a video introduction for each word
◀)) **Listen** to iWords
📖 **Refer** to the online dictionary

1. recreation
(rek-ree-AY-shuhn)

(n.) A fun or relaxing activity is something you do for *recreation*.

2. minimum
(MIN-uh-muhm)

(n.) If you had to score a *minimum* of 70 to pass a test, you would fail if you scored 69. *Minimum* refers to the least possible.

3. maximum
(MAK-suh-muhm)

(n.) If you can carry a *maximum* of two bags on an airplane for free, you would be charged if you had three. *Maximum* refers to the most possible.

4. likewise
(LIKE-wize)

(adv.) When you want to say that another example is similar to the first, or to mean "in addition," you can include the word "*likewise.*" For instance: I enjoy eating oranges and *likewise* most citrus fruits.

5. photosynthesis
(foh-toh-SIN-thuh-siss)

(n.) When sunlight combines with elements in a plant cell to produce chlorophyll, which supports plant life, the process is called *photosynthesis*.

6. energy
(EN-ur-jee)

(n.) Usable power that can take many forms but provides the force to get work done or the fuel for a process is called *energy*.

(n.) Being active mentally and physically calls upon and displays *energy*.

7. ecosystem
(EE-koh-siss-tuhm)

(n.) When you refer to a group or community of living things that depend on each other, how they interact, and their surroundings, you are discussing an *ecosystem*.

8. factor
(FAK-tur)

(n.) Any element that contributes to an end result is a *factor* or a part.

(v.) When you contribute to or are involved in an outcome, you *factor* into the final product.

9. benefit
(BEN-uh-fit)

(v.) When you are given an advantage, you *benefit* from it.

(n.) Something that promotes well-being is a *benefit*. If you receive a *benefit* from someone or something, you are getting help in a good way.

10. prone
(prohn)

(adj.) If you are unlikely to remember names, you are *prone* to forget, or have a tendency to forget.

(adv.) If you are lying flat, or face-down, you are lying *prone*.

Word Talk

Each lesson word has been placed in a category. With a partner, discuss and list items that belong in each category. Compare your results with those of another pair of students.

Living Things That Undergo *Photosynthesis*	Activities We Do for *Recreation*

Items That Can Be Filled to Their *Maximum*	How to *Benefit* from Exercise	*Factors* That Influence Your Grades	Sources of *Energy*

Ecosystems You Can Visit	The *Minimum* You Need for Specific Activities	Sentences That Include the Word *"Likewise"*	Information You Are *Prone* to Forget

Check for Understanding

Choose the lesson word that completes each sentence. Write the word on the line provided. Some words will be used twice.

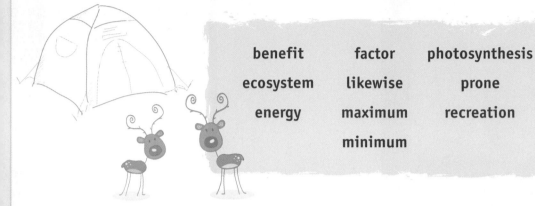

benefit	factor	photosynthesis
ecosystem	likewise	prone
energy	maximum	recreation
	minimum	

1. Darla pushed herself to the _____ because she hoped to win the race.

2. Tall plants _____ by getting more sunlight, but strong winds are a danger to them.

3. My dog is _____ to howl when she hears a car alarm go off nearby.

4. A rusted support column was a major _____ in the bridge's collapse.

5. Experts warn that we should conserve _____ such as electricity and gas.

6. Some elements of our _____ include plants, water, and mammals.

7. For _____ I like to go camping, but Alicia thinks camping is punishment.

8. Ariel's donation is the _____ that the charity requests, because it's all she can afford.

9. The storm left a heavy coating of dust on the leaves of the trees, which kept _____ from occurring.

10. People like to have contact with others; _____, they need friends.

11. Keisha's enthusiasm was an important _____ in helping our team win, even though she could not play because of her injury.

12. _____ in the form of sunlight provides food for plants and a source of fuel for people.

Expand Word Meanings

Read the paragraph below to learn other meanings for some of the lesson words.

Can you believe that someday you may drive a car powered by pond scum? One of the most unusual fuel sources developed in recent years comes from the green algae that live on the surface of ponds. Scientists using new technology can factor sunlight, water, and carbon dioxide into a chemical process that produces a sugar. Then the algae convert the sugar into oil. If you are now lying prone in shock and disbelief, gather your energy. There is more! Scientists also found another benefit to using algae. They say algae actually remove dangerous pollutants from the atmosphere.

> **!** Notice that the meanings of these words differ from the way they were first used in the lesson. The noun and verb forms of *factor* and *benefit* are closely related in meaning. *Prone*, however, refers to a literal position, not a tendency. The meaning of *energy* here is not scientific, although its other meaning is.

Apply Other Meanings

Complete each sentence with a highlighted word from the paragraph above.

1. One _____ of being tall is that you can change lightbulbs without using a ladder.

2. I learned to swim in a/an _____ position, but I love to do the backstroke now.

3. A quarterback will _____ in the wind speed when deciding where to throw the football.

4. After running the marathon, Han had no _____ left.

5. Many people sleep in a/an _____ position because they tend to snore if they sleep face-up.

6. Nine hours of sleep will give me enough _____ to do well on tomorrow's test.

7. The class picnic was postponed because we forgot to _____ in the possibility of rain that day.

8. Our class raised money, gathered contributions, and volunteered time for the _____ of people who lost their homes in a fire.

9. We did push-ups while _____, and then we did leg lifts while lying on our backs.

10. Shania felt that spending a day helping to build houses for the homeless was a/an _____, not a drawback, of the program.

LESSON 13

Word Associations

Use what you know about the lesson word in italics to answer each question. Circle the letter next to the phrase that best answers the question. Be prepared to explain your answers.

1. Which effort would require the greatest amount of *energy*?

   a. adding wood to a big fire
   b. running twenty miles
   c. filling up a gas tank

2. Which process involves *photosynthesis*?

   a. making electricity from sunlight
   b. taking a picture with a camera
   c. a plant turning green in the sun

3. In which activity would someone be *prone*?

   a. sleeping
   b. eating
   c. cleaning

4. Which phrase could you use instead of *likewise* to list reasons?

   a. from another point of view
   b. in addition
   c. on the other hand

5. Which capacity is at *maximum*?

   a. a half-full bucket
   b. an overflowing sink
   c. a full tank of gas

6. Which setting could be considered an *ecosystem*?

   a. an empty gym
   b. a parking lot
   c. a pond

7. Which element could be a major *factor* in the failure of a dam?

   a. the age of the structure
   b. a light rainfall the previous year
   c. people using water to bathe

8. Which of these amounts might be the *minimum* needed to stay alive?

   a. three meals a day
   b. two bottles of water
   c. nine hours of sleep

9. Which activity would most people consider to be *recreation*?

   a. painting their bathroom
   b. walking with a friend
   c. studying for a test

10. Which of the following would be considered a *benefit* from exercise?

    a. good health
    b. sore muscles
    c. a minor injury

148

Check Again

Use what you know about the lesson word in italics to complete each sentence. Be sure your sentences make sense.

1. If you want a group to *benefit* from a charity, you _____ _____

2. If you said, "Cats play with toys," you could begin your next sentence: "*Likewise*, dogs _____ _____

3. If I listed ways I use *energy* every day, one item would be _____

4. The *maximum* that I usually eat in a day is _____

5. If one part of an *ecosystem* changes, the other parts _____

6. After I paint my room, I will need some *recreation* so I will _____ _____

7. To lie *prone* in the bed, _____

8. When you pack supplies for a picnic, *factor* in _____ _____

9. As you walk through the forest, you know *photosynthesis* is at work if you see _____ _____

10. The *minimum* required to be a good friend is _____

Challenge Yourself

Follow the directions to write sentences with the lesson words in italics. Be sure your sentences make sense both grammatically and in meaning.

1. Write a sentence with *benefit* in the fifth position.

2. Write a question with the word *minimum* in the fifth position.

3. Write a sentence exactly fifteen words in length using the word *prone*.

Word-Solving Strategies:
Context Clues

Antonyms

Often, authors provide contrast by using antonyms of words. Read this sentence from "Miraculous Seaweed":

Scientists estimate that there are a minimum of 1,000 to a maximum of 10,000 kinds of seaweed.

The text says 1,000 is the **minimum**, the least amount, and 10,000 is the **maximum**, the greatest number. *Least* and *greatest* are opposites, so **maximum** and **minimum** are antonyms.

BE CAREFUL!

Words may sometimes seem like antonyms when they really are not. Read this sentence:

Humans benefit from seaweed while fish disguise themselves in it.

The verbs *benefit* and *disguise* are not antonyms. *Suffer* is an antonym of *benefit*. *Reveal* is an antonym of *disguise*.

Practice

A. Write the vocabulary word and its antonym in the first two boxes. Use context clues to write another meaning for the word in the third box.

In the past, some energy executives tried to stop the development of new types of energy. Now, fresh ideas have begun to stimulate scientists to find more energy without destroying our planet. Fuel cells were first accepted as workable, but then discarded as impractical. Coal was an original heat source. Later, it wasn't used as much, although recently it has become an alternative to oil. Some of the studies about coal's use reached accurate conclusions. Others published faulty results.

WORD	ANTONYM	WORD MEANING

B. Write a sentence for each of the highlighted words from the paragraph above. Include an antonym as a context clue.

1. _____

2. _____

3. _____

4. _____

Practice for Tests

Fill in the bubble next to the answer that best completes the sentence or answers the question.

1. Read this sentence.

   Jorge loves bowling; *likewise,* he appreciates the opera.

   Likewise means:
   - ○ **A** additionally
   - ○ **B** usually
   - ○ **C** occasionally
   - ○ **D** strangely

2. When you *benefit* from something, it:
   - ○ **A** costs you some money
   - ○ **B** makes your clothes fit better
   - ○ **C** forces you to reconsider
   - ○ **D** makes you better off

3. The opposite of *minimum* is:
   - ○ **A** the least
   - ○ **B** the middle
   - ○ **C** the most
   - ○ **D** the average

4. In which group would all things be part of the same *ecosystem*?
   - ○ **A** coral, fish, octopus
   - ○ **B** squirrel, hawk, penguin
   - ○ **C** whale, worm, dog
   - ○ **D** llama, frog, dolphin

5. A word NOT associated with *photosynthesis* is:
   - ○ **A** sunlight
   - ○ **B** plant
   - ○ **C** animals
   - ○ **D** food

6. Read this sentence.

   Plants and people need *energy* to live and grow.

   Energy means:
   - ○ **A** gasoline
   - ○ **B** power
   - ○ **C** strength
   - ○ **D** food

7. When the cost reaches the *maximum*, it:
   - ○ **A** is affordable
   - ○ **B** cannot go any higher
   - ○ **C** is less than it should be
   - ○ **D** is hardly anything at all

8. When you *factor* in a condition, you:
   - ○ **A** consider it
   - ○ **B** become emotional about it
   - ○ **C** turn it into an opinion
   - ○ **D** ignore it

9. You would most likely assume a *prone* position to:
   - ○ **A** climb a tall tree safely
   - ○ **B** give a talk in class
   - ○ **C** look at earth worms in the soil
   - ○ **D** do a headstand in a yoga class

10. A person engaged in *recreation* might:
   - ○ **A** work on a difficult task
   - ○ **B** play a game
   - ○ **C** start a job
   - ○ **D** go to sleep

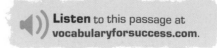
▶ **Watch** a video introduction to this passage at **vocabularyforsuccess.com**.

🔊 **Listen** to this passage at **vocabularyforsuccess.com**.

The Dirt Under Your Feet
<magazine article>

Did you know that the dirt beneath your feet is teeming with life?

When you step outside by yourself, you probably think you're alone. You're not. In the dirt below your feet are billions of living organisms that are *very* important.

Bacteria Bacteria are single-celled organisms. Some cause infection and make us sick. However, most are helpful, including those underground. Scientists suggest that a teaspoon of dirt may contain a billion bacteria. They're part of a category of living things that help decompose dead plant and animal material. One consequence of this process is that the nutrients in this dead matter are recycled. The dead material is broken apart and returned to the dirt, and ultimately it feeds the plants and animals.

Fungi A fungus is also a single-celled organism. There are almost as many fungi below our feet as there are bacteria. Often you can find one that acts like a parasite, feeding off the roots of a plant. That fungus also benefits the plant that acts as its host by helping the plant absorb water and nutrients.

Worms Some worms seek bacteria and fungi to eat. These worms are so small—nearly microscopic—that a handful of soil may

Bacteria

Earthworms

~ **VOCABULARY** ~

infection	parasite
category	host
decompose	seek
consequence	consume
fungus	impact

contain thousands of them. Other worms, however, are larger but equally plentiful. An acre of land may contain a million or more earthworms. As they consume an estimated ten tons of dead plant material, these earthworms break apart the soil so more oxygen and water can reach living plants. The impact of worms on soil and crop development is enormous.

Other Critters Insects, spiders, snakes, mice, and moles are also found underground. Along with bacteria, fungi, and worms, they help form an intricate underground food chain. Creatures eat other creatures, which are in turn eaten by other creatures. Just like most food chains on Earth, this underground chain starts with plants and the microbes that help them grow.

TALK ABOUT IT

With a partner, answer the questions below. Use as many of the highlighted words in the selection as you can.

1. **What would happen if nothing were ever to *decompose*?**

2. **What might be a *consequence* of placing earthworms in your garden?**

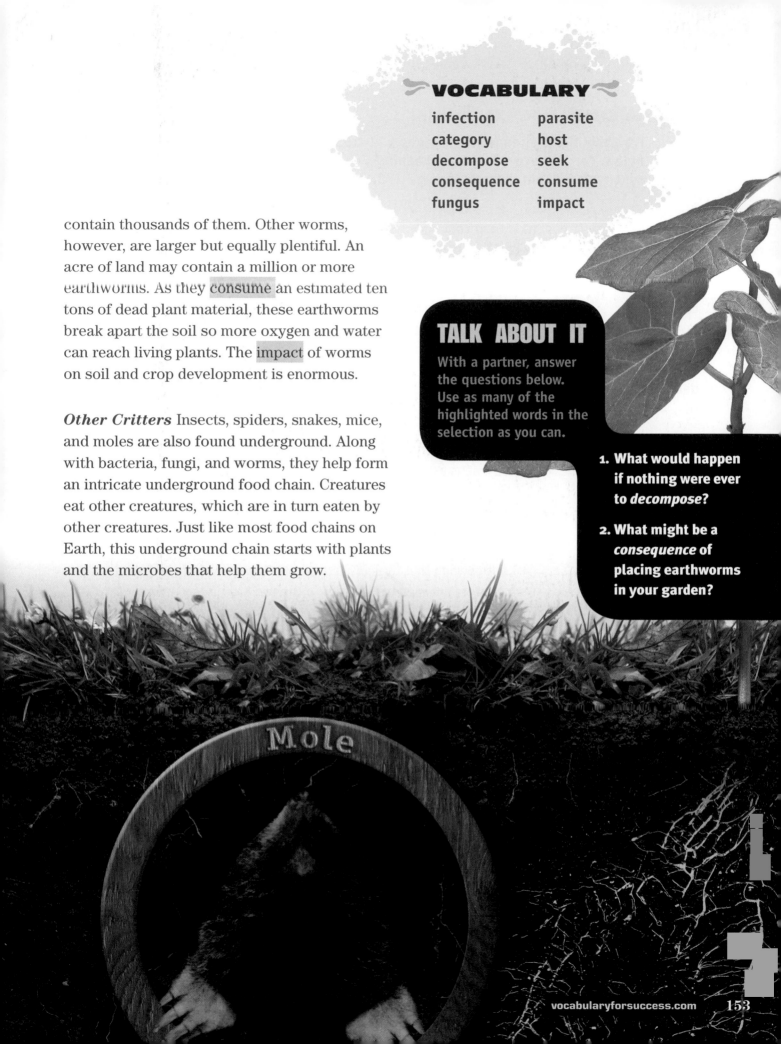

Mole

vocabularyforsuccess.com
▶ **Watch** a video introduction for each word
◀)) **Listen** to iWords
📖 **Refer** to the online dictionary

Word Meanings

For each highlighted word on pages 152–153, the meaning is given below. For practice with other meanings, see pages 157–159. For synonyms and antonyms, see page 172.

1. infection
(in-FEK-shuhn)

(n.) When your body has an *infection*, germs or bacteria have attacked your healthy cells, making you sick.

2. category
(KAT-uh-gor-ee)

(n.) When you organize a group of different things, you gather those that are alike in some way into a *category* or group.

3. decompose
(dee-kuhm-POZE)

(v.) When garbage breaks down or rots, it will *decompose* or decay.

4. consequence
(KON-suh-kwenss)

(n.) One *consequence* of not cleaning up your room is that you will begin to lose things as a result of the mess.

5. fungus
(FUHN-guhss)

(n.) A *fungus* is a plant-like organism that has no leaves, flowers, roots, or chlorophyll. A *fungus* feeds off the material on which it grows.

6. parasite
(PA-ruh-site)

(n.) A tapeworm that lives inside a dog is a *parasite* because it steals from another animal what it needs to survive.

(n.) If someone lives off your money and kindness, he or she can be called a *parasite*.

7. host
(hohst)

(n.) A *host* is an animal or plant on which another animal or plant feeds.

(v.) To offer food and entertainment at your own party is to *host* an event.

8. seek
(seek)

(v.) When you look for something, you *seek* something that is unknown or lost.

9. consume
(kuhn-soom)

(v.) When you *consume* food, you eat it.

(v.) A fire is said to *consume* a house if the fire destroys the whole house.

10. impact
(IM-pakt)

(n.) Changes have an *impact* or major effect on your plans.

(v.) Good fortune will *impact* your life because it will affect the way you live, and make a difference.

Word Talk

Each lesson word is listed here. With a partner, take turns drawing a picture to illustrate the meaning of six of the words. As one partner draws, the other partner identifies the vocabulary word.

category

consequence

consume

decompose

fungus

host (n.)

impact (n.)

infection

parasite

seek

consume

Check for Understanding

Choose the lesson word that completes each sentence. Write the word on the line provided. Some words will be used twice.

category	decompose	infection
consequence	fungus	parasite
consume	host	seek
	impact	

1. After my mother found a/an _____ on our cat, she bought a tick collar to protect him from others.

2. The dogs will _____, in fact gobble up wildly, their new dog food.

3. The judges had to invent a new _____ for your entry, because it didn't fit any of the other groups they had created.

4. The horse has a bad _____ on its hoof, which was very red and sore.

5. After the food scraps _____ in the garden, they'll help the plants grow.

6. A pine tree can be a/an _____ for insects, which can live in the tree's bark or feed on the tree's sap.

7. My father told me that if you _____ the truth, you will always find it.

8. As a/an _____ of the boy's poor preparation, he lost the race.

9. A virus grows inside of a/an _____, which it needs in order to survive.

10. Like yeast and mildew, mold is a/an _____ that lives in wet places.

11. At breakfast we will _____ eggs, potatoes, bread, and fruit.

12. Winning "most improved player" at the softball awards ceremony had a positive _____ on my confidence.

Expand Word Meanings

Read the paragraph below to learn other meanings for some of the lesson words.

Our neighbor, Clyde, is always telling us how to grow fruits and vegetables in our garden. Unfortunately, my mother says he is a parasite, because he never plants his own garden. Instead, he helps himself to our food. He also likes to host parties. Guess whose fruits and vegetables he serves? Ours! That's not all. During the winter, he takes wood from our shed. On cold nights, he burns log after log, and we fear he will consume our entire wood supply. One day my mother built a tall fence around our property. She knew this would impact Clyde's life, but she was tired of the way his selfishness had affected our life.

> **!** Notice that the meanings of the highlighted words here are similar to those that you learned earlier in the lesson. A person can be called a *parasite* when, like the creatures in nature, they take advantage of others. People *consume* food when they eat, while a fireplace can *consume* many logs.

Apply Other Meanings

Complete each sentence with a highlighted word from the paragraph above.

1. If you want to _____ the work of the student government, you can run for school office.

2. Donnell wanted to give a party, but he was not sure how to _____ such a large event.

3. Ocean waves can _____ a sand castle in a matter of seconds.

4. When Uncle Raul lived with my family, he helped out with chores and paid rent, rather than being a/an _____ who lived in the house for free.

5. Our principal decided to _____ a celebration to show his appreciation for our efforts in organizing the after-school classes.

6. Residents hoped the forest fire would not _____ the entire woodlands.

7. "You can not be a/an _____ in this country!" the politician told the voters. "You must pay taxes in exchange for government services."

8. The high cost of equipment will _____ the organization's budget.

9. The flood victims watched the raging river _____ the house and carry it away.

10. Our school will _____ foreign students who who want to study in this country.

Word Associations

Use what you know about the lesson word in italics to answer each question. Circle the letter next to the phrase that best answers the question. Be prepared to explain your answers.

1. Which object would *decompose* fastest?

   a. plastic
   b. vegetable peels
   c. an animal bone

2. Which of these might you *seek* if you were lost?

   a. food
   b. your home
   c. the wind

3. Which event might someone *host*?

   a. an awards show
   b. a holiday
   c. a graduation

4. Which of these could *consume* your happiness?

   a. sunshine
   b. anger
   c. bread

5. Which of these word pairs contain things that belong in the same *category*?

   a. toys, games, puzzles
   b. dogs, cats, books
   c. ice, blue, winter

6. Which of these traits would a *parasite* lack?

   a. greed
   b. pushiness
   c. independence

7. What could you use to fight against *infection*?

   a. soap and water
   b. bow and arrow
   c. surgery and transplants

8. Where is a good place for a *fungus* to live?

   a. in a clean hospital room
   b. on fallen leaves in a forest
   c. on an ice cube in the freezer

9. Which of the following would have a powerful *impact*?

   a. a little misunderstanding
   b. a major change
   c. nothing important

10. Which of these facts might be a *consequence* of a slip on the ice?

    a. broken wrist
    b. new skates
    c. being thirsty

Check Again

Use what you know about the lesson word in italics to complete each sentence. Be sure your sentences make sense.

1. After people *consume* a meal at a restaurant, they _____

2. Jess turned to a computer search engine to *seek* _____

3. A *consequence* of spraining your ankle might include _____

4. When the peach in our fruit bowl began to *decompose*, _____

5. A sign of an *infection* in a body might be _____

6. The money the track team raised at the car wash will *impact* _____
   _____

7. If you leave cheese out of the refrigerator, *fungus* will cause mold to _____
   _____

8. In the baking competition, my apple pie won in the "best all-around" *category*, so _____
   _____

9. A *parasite* can harm another animal by _____

10. When you *host* a party, you have to _____
    _____

Challenge Yourself

Write Your Own

Follow the directions to write sentences with the lesson words in italics. Be sure your sentences make sense both grammatically and in meaning.

1. Write a sentence with *parasite* in the fifth position.

2. Write a sentence exactly ten words in length with *host* in the fifth position.

3. Write a sentence using the word *fungus* that discusses its role in nature.

LESSON

14 Word-Solving Strategies: Context Clues

Inferences

Sometimes a text does not contain all the information readers need in order to understand a word's meaning. Readers have to make inferences to understand unknown words. Read this sentence from "The Dirt Under Your Feet."

> One consequence of this process is that the nutrients in this dead matter are recycled.

After the word **consequence,** the author describes what happens. The reader can infer that a **consequence** is a *result*.

BE CAREFUL!

If a sentence does not have words that help you make an inference, use what you know about a topic to figure out unknown words or phrases. Read this sentence: *"This food chain starts with plants and the microbes that help them grow."* **To understand this concept you would already need to know what a microbe is, or consult a dictionary.**

Practice

A. Write a highlighted word and an inference clue in the first two boxes. Then write another meaning for the word in the third box.

> Moles accomplish a lot with only their small arms and compact bodies. They have a special manner of digging. They press their arms out to either side. This motion produces powerful forces. Their dense bone and muscle arrangement helps them move with a force that is equal to 32 times their weight. Close examination has shown that a five-ounce mole can dig an 18-foot-long tunnel in an hour.

WORD	INFERENCE CLUE	WORD MEANING

B. Write a sentence for each of the highlighted words from the paragraph above. Use a thesaurus to find words with similar meanings to help you create inferences.

1. _____

   _____

2. _____

   _____

160

Practice for Tests

Fill in the bubble next to the answer that best completes the sentence or answers the question.

1. Read this sentence.

   People eat bread made with yeast, a type of *fungus* that makes bread rise.

   Fungus means:
   - ○ **A** a plantlike creature
   - ○ **B** a very tiny insect
   - ○ **C** germs that can harm us
   - ○ **D** elements found only underground

2. When you *consume* something, you:
   - ○ **A** eat it up
   - ○ **B** share it
   - ○ **C** catch it in your hand
   - ○ **D** step on it

3. A *consequence* of overeating might be:
   - ○ **A** a toothache
   - ○ **B** a grin
   - ○ **C** a stomachache
   - ○ **D** a cold

4. In which group can all the items be described as something a bird will *seek*?
   - ○ **A** a pond, insects, crumbs
   - ○ **B** a mate, shelter, a book
   - ○ **C** a cave, worms, a shell
   - ○ **D** a tree, safety, money

5. A word closely associated with *host* is:
   - ○ **A** attend
   - ○ **B** unwelcome
   - ○ **C** organize
   - ○ **D** timid

6. Read this sentence.

   The apple will *decompose* quickly if it is left out in the sun.

   Decompose means:
   - ○ **A** get fresher
   - ○ **B** become ripe
   - ○ **C** grow from it
   - ○ **D** begin to rot

7. A *parasite* is:
   - ○ **A** a furry pet
   - ○ **B** a contributor
   - ○ **C** a troublemaker
   - ○ **D** an animal that lives off another

8. Something is put in a *category* if it is:
   - ○ **A** a group
   - ○ **B** a division of a larger group
   - ○ **C** the title of a whole movement
   - ○ **D** exactly like everything else

9. You know you have an *infection* when:
   - ○ **A** you can't walk
   - ○ **B** you feel pain and slightly sick
   - ○ **C** your body is healthy
   - ○ **D** you have to go to an office

10. When things *impact* each other, they:
    - ○ **A** affect each other
    - ○ **B** get along
    - ○ **C** hardly communicate
    - ○ **D** are broken

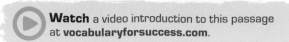
▶ **Watch** a video introduction to this passage at **vocabularyforsuccess.com**.

🔊 **Listen** to this passage at **vocabularyforsuccess.com**.

Conserving Our Resources

\<letter to the editor\>

Dear Editor:

I'm angry! Every day I hear conversations about the environment. Some people fear we will deplete our energy resources, which causes a decline in animal and plant species. Others complain that our environment continues to degenerate. Many people say these problems are so big, only governments can solve them. However, I believe that change must start somewhere, so I ask, why not start with each of us? Here's my plan.

This vehicle runs on recycled cooking oil.

Think reuse. Recycling is not just about bottles and cans; it's also about finding creative new uses for what we might otherwise throw away. Every year, restaurants discard millions of gallons of used cooking oil. Now some very clever people are collecting copious amounts of it, and transforming it into fuel for cars.

Think outside the box. If you've flown a kite, you know that sometimes it seems as if there's no wind. However, if you fly your kite high enough, you will always detect a wind current. One climate scientist says that wind power is such an abundant energy source, it is capable of providing more energy than the world needs. We need to find the best way to capture it. Some scientists are experimenting with harnessing wind power from huge kites that would fly high up in the sky.

Think big.
When singer Taja Sevelle was just 17, she had a hit song. Then, while recording more music in Detroit, she noticed that hunger had begun to invade the city. *Why not grow food on vacant lots?* she wondered. Growing locally helps people and is an excellent way to save energy. In 2005, Taja and the group she started, Urban Farming, began growing three gardens. Now Urban Farming has 160 gardens around the country, and they believe their simple idea can foster big change—the end of world hunger.

I challenge everyone to go beyond the simple critique offered here. When you wake up tomorrow, ask how you can help the world!

Signed,

P. Knapp

VOCABULARY

deplete	copious
decline	detect
species	invade
degenerate	foster
recycling	critique

TALK ABOUT IT

With a partner, answer the questions below. Use as many of the highlighted words in the selection as you can.

1. What kinds of *recycling* do you and your community do? Describe.

2. Give a brief *critique* of this passage. Offer a detailed argument for or against this plan.

Word Meanings

vocabularyforsuccess.com
▶ **Watch** a video introduction for each word
◀)) **Listen** to iWords
📖 **Refer** to the online dictionary

For each highlighted word on pages 162-163, the meaning is given below. For practice with other meanings, see pages 167–169. For synonyms and antonyms, see page 172.

1. deplete
(di-PLEET)

(v.) When you *deplete* a supply, you use up or spend all of it.

2. decline
(di-KLINE)

(n.) Something that experiences a *decline* has a drop or a loss.

(v.) If something were to *decline*, it would be decreasing or losing in some way.

3. species
(SPEE-sheez)

(n.) Two living things are of the same *species* or classification if their characteristics are similar enough to produce offspring.

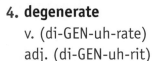

4. degenerate
v. (di-GEN-uh-rate)
adj. (di-GEN-uh-rit)

(v.) If something begins to *degenerate*, it gets weaker and falls apart.

(adj.) When you describe something as *degenerate*, you are saying it has fallen into a low mental or physical state.

5. recycling
(ree-SYE-kleeng)

(n.) When you participate in *recycling*, you reuse or break something down so it can be reprocessed.

6. copious
(KOH-pee-uhs)

(n.) When you have *copious* amounts of something, you have more than enough or even an overflowing supply.

7. detect
(dee-TEKT)

(v.) When you *detect* something, you discover or notice it.

8. invade
(in-VADE)

(v.) When something manages to *invade* a place, it enters and spreads throughout it, often in a harmful way.

9. foster
(FAW-stur)

(v.) When you *foster* something, you encourage and support it.

(adj.) *Foster* parents are people who care for a child as parents do, often temporarily, and who are not related by blood.

10. critique
(kri-TEEK)

(n.) A written criticism or analysis of something is called a *critique*.

(v.) When you evaluate or examine something, you *critique* it.

Word Talk

Each lesson word has been placed in a category. With a partner, discuss and list items that belong in each category. Compare your results with those of another pair of students.

Things You Would Write a *Critique* About	Things That *Degenerate*

Ways We Can *Detect* Things in the Dark	Things That Come Packaged in *Copious* Amounts	Ways to *Foster* Friendship	Things That Someone Can *Deplete*

Places and Things Bugs *Invade*	Living Things That Are in the Same *Species*	Examples of *Recycling*	Things That Show a *Decline* in Number

Check for Understanding

Choose the lesson word that completes each sentence. Write the word on the line provided. Some words will be used twice.

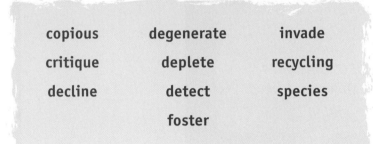

copious	degenerate	invade
critique	deplete	recycling
decline	detect	species
	foster	

1. A large bin for _____ cans and bottles is beside the garbage cans.

2. _____ amounts of apples fall off our tree and cover the ground.

3. People talking loudly and failing to respect others point to a/an _____ in good manners.

4. The condition of the house continued to _____ after the porch collapsed and the roof leaked and nothing was repaired.

5. After the play, the reviewer wrote a/an _____ of the acting.

6. If you _____ any movement on the pond's surface, it is probably only the wind.

7. There are so many strawberries in the garden this year, it will be hard to _____ all the fruit on the plants.

8. Some of the 233 primate _____ include baboons, gorillas, and lemurs.

9. When grasshoppers _____ a cornfield, they can destroy the crop in just a few days.

10. Our principal will _____ goodwill by promoting "Compliment Day."

11. The student newspaper published a favorable _____ of the art show.

12. _____ is one good way to help clean up the planet.

Expand Word Meanings

Read the paragraph below to learn other meanings for some of the lesson words.

Young artists often look for an older artist who will act as a kind of foster parent, or mentor. These role models can help them succeed in the art world by giving them good advice and introducing them to important people. Older artists benefit, too. They are eager to pass along their knowledge before their skills begin to decline. As artists age, their skills or senses may become degenerate, and that can affect their art. But there are also benefits to aging. Older artists' life experiences help them cope. They may think of past successes when others critique their new work. Young artists benefit when they witness such confidence.

! Readers may be unfamiliar with some of the secondary meanings used here. Look at the meanings on page 164 and notice the relationship between the words' different parts of speech. Something that is *degenerate* has *degenerated*. You can link the meanings of many words to their more common usages.

Apply Other Meanings

Complete each sentence with a highlighted word from the paragraph above.

1. Students sometimes have a hard time when their peers _____ their writing.

2. Often, children without families will live in a _____ home before they are permanently adopted by a new parent.

3. Your grades will _____ if you don't do your homework.

4. A _____ water pipe burst and flooded the room, so it must be replaced.

5. I asked my mother to _____ the cookies I made so I could improve the recipe and make them even more delicious.

6. The number of lightning bolts began to _____, then quickly increased again as the rain poured down.

7. Many _____ owners provide care and love for stray pets before they are adopted by new owners.

8. In crime movies there is often a _____ character who breaks the laws and is mean to others.

9. Karen didn't want to _____ the song until she'd listened to it several times.

10. The animal rescue found _____ families for dogs and cats that needed temporary homes.

Word Associations

Use what you know about the lesson word in italics to answer each question. Circle the letter next to the phrase that best answers the question. Be prepared to explain your answers.

1. Which of these is easiest to *detect*?

   a. a faint scent

   b. a loud noise

   c. a hidden animal

2. Which word describes something *copious*?

   a. unique

   b. lonely

   c. plentiful

3. Which document could be described as a *critique*?

   a. a book review

   b. a love letter

   c. a news story

4. Which would help *foster* confidence?

   a. stumbling

   b. encouragement

   c. yelling

5. Which is an example of *recycling*?

   a. planting trees

   b. building houses

   c. reusing bottles

6. Which activity is likely to cause a person's health to *degenerate*?

   a. exercise

   b. enough sleep

   c. poor nutrition

7. Which location would help an army to *invade*?

   a. a thick, dark forest

   b. a large, flat field

   c. an endless grassy plain

8. Which resource would be hardest to *deplete*?

   a. gas for cars

   b. air to breathe

   c. clothes to wear

9. Which characteristic are all *species* of tigers known for?

   a. their vegetarian diet

   b. being predators

   c. living in zoos

10. Which product has seen a *decline* in use over the past few years?

    a. CD players

    b. cell phones

    c. computers

Check Again

Use what you know about the lesson word in italics to complete each sentence. Be sure your sentences make sense.

1. If you wrote a *critique* of someone's singing, you might say _____

_____

2. To *foster* growth in houseplants, you should _____

3. If you dug a hole and found *copious* pieces of gold, you would _____

4. If you noticed a sharp *decline* in the amount your pet ate, you might _____

5. When a person's health begins to *degenerate*, _____

6. In order to *detect* birds on a bird-watching hike, people will _____

_____

7. When mosquitoes *invade* your tent while camping, you can _____

8. *Recycling* helps the whole world because it _____

_____

9. Scientists group similar animals into *species* in order to _____

_____

10. If an art club managed to *deplete* all its supplies, its members would _____

_____

Challenge Yourself

Write Your Own

Follow the directions to write sentences with the lesson words in italics. Be sure your sentences make sense both grammatically and in meaning.

1. Write a sentence with the word *copious* in the second position.

2. Write a sentence exactly eight words in length using the word *invade*.

3. Write a question using the word *detect* in the fourth position.

Word-Solving Strategies: Prefixes

The prefix de-: "un," "off," "away"

Many prefixes add meaning to their root words. For example, *bi-* (two) joins with *cycle* (wheel) to form *bicycle*, or a vehicle with two wheels.

The prefix *de-*, which means "un," "off," or "away," functions differently. It changes the meaning of its root, often completely reversing it. In the lesson word *degenerate*, the base word, *generate*, means "to create, build, or grow." When we add the prefix *de-*, the new word means the opposite. Something that *degenerates* falls apart.

The same process occurs for the word *deplete*. In Latin, *plere* means "to fill." When we add the prefix *de-*, we get *deplete*, which means "to empty." For the lesson word *detect*, the Latin root word is *tegere*, meaning

"to cover." When the *de-* is added, it means *off*, or the opposite of cover. To detect is to uncover—to notice or discover. If you want to see how the prefix *de-* alters a word's meaning, examine its root or base word.

Examples

When the prefix *de-* is added to these root words, their meanings are reversed.

cide (*caedere*: to cut) → decide

feat (*facere*: to do) → defeat

fine (*finis*: end) → define

spair (*desperare*: hope) → despair

hydrate → dehydrate

caffeinate → decaffeinate

BE CAREFUL!

Not all words that start with *de-* have a prefix that means "un," "off," or "away." Consider the words *deer, delicious,* and *dead*. In the sentence *The food is delicious*, there is no "un," "off," or "away" message. Remember, many words share the same letters as those built with a prefix. Always consider the context, make inferences, or check a dictionary to be sure.

Practice

Use what you've learned about the prefix *de-* to create words that mean the opposite or nearly the opposite of the given words.

1. form _____

2. code _____

3. tour _____

4. compress _____

5. classify _____

6. value _____

7. camp _____

8. humidify _____

9. bug _____

10. magnetize _____

Practice for Tests

Fill in the bubble next to the answer that best completes the sentence or answers the question.

1. Read this sentence.

    When bacteria *invade* your blood, the immune system attacks.

    Invade means:
    - ○ **A** break into
    - ○ **B** escape from
    - ○ **C** drip on
    - ○ **D** reduce

2. A conversation can *degenerate* when:
    - ○ **A** people are listening
    - ○ **B** two people agree
    - ○ **C** people talk loudly
    - ○ **D** too many people talk at once

3. The opposite of *decline* is:
    - ○ **A** shrink
    - ○ **B** vary
    - ○ **C** multiply
    - ○ **D** fight

4. In which group could none of the items be found in *copious* amounts?
    - ○ **A** dinosaurs, rare flowers, pandas
    - ○ **B** stars, clouds, dreams
    - ○ **C** skyscrapers, highways, islands
    - ○ **D** oranges, pencils, writers

5. A word closely associated with *foster* is:
    - ○ **A** cousin
    - ○ **B** respond
    - ○ **C** help
    - ○ **D** quicker

6. Read this sentence.

    The rain forest has an incredible number of different *species*.

    Species means:
    - ○ **A** special challenges
    - ○ **B** wet environments
    - ○ **C** tropical plants
    - ○ **D** animal and plant groups

7. A car is *degenerate* if it is:
    - ○ **A** extremely fast
    - ○ **B** falling apart
    - ○ **C** very rare
    - ○ **D** part of a group

8. When you *deplete* a supply, it does NOT:
    - ○ **A** stay the same
    - ○ **B** get smaller
    - ○ **C** need to be refilled
    - ○ **D** get near the end

9. In which job would you try to *detect* the source of a problem?
    - ○ **A** dancer
    - ○ **B** poet
    - ○ **C** investigator
    - ○ **D** robber

10. A person writing a *critique* would:
    - ○ **A** explain how to do something
    - ○ **B** express an opinion
    - ○ **C** tell a good story
    - ○ **D** create unforgettable characters

Synonyms and Antonyms

In the following Word Bank, you will find synonyms and antonyms for some of the words in Lessons 13–15. (Remember: Some words have both synonyms and antonyms.) Study these words; then complete the exercises below.

starve	delicate	suffer	expand	eagerness	decay
enhance	discourage	cause	amusement	meager	pursue

A. For each sentence, fill in the blank with a SYNONYM for the word in boldface.

1. The police tried to _____ the criminal until a tornado forced them to **seek** shelter.

2. Although I'm upset that my tennis match is canceled because of the heavy rain, I know the moisture will **benefit** the plants and _____ the appearance of the town.

3. Studies have shown that some garbage will not _____ for decades, while other materials **decompose** quickly.

4. Henry runs on the beach for **recreation**, but his dogs trot along just for their _____.

5. A desire for progress is a/an _____ for change in any election, but another key **factor** is the voter's need to feel like a part of the process.

B. For each sentence, fill in the blank with an ANTONYM for the word in boldface.

6. Despite the _____ number of people attending the event, the hosts seemed to offer **copious** amounts of meat and fruit.

7. Hungry animals will **consume** plants they don't enjoy eating rather than _____.

8. People watering their lawns during the drought will **deplete** the water supply so much that the city will have to _____ the ban on watering lawns.

9. A good coach can **foster** a winning attitude even if frequent losses _____ the players.

10. Alternative energy sources can **benefit** the environment. Can you think of any group that would _____ if we stopped using the current forms of energy?

Word Study: Idioms

An **idiom** is a phrase that means something different from the literal meaning of its words. For example, if someone asks if "a cat's got your tongue," she doesn't want to know if a cat is playing with your tongue. She is asking in a humorous way why you are so quiet when she thinks you should be talking.

The meanings of many of the words in Lessons 13–15 suggest possible idioms. For example, you might say that a friend will have to "pay the piper" if he decides to do something that would result in a negative consequence (Lesson 14) if he's caught.

Practice

Read each sentence. Use context clues to figure out the meaning of each idiom in boldface. Then, write the letter of the definition for the idiom.

_____ 1. That family is always getting something new in their effort to **keep up with the Joneses**.

_____ 2. The star athlete was content to **rest on his laurels** when all he does is talk about the races he won a long time ago.

_____ 3. You are **comparing apples to oranges** when you talk about the differences between a sports car and a minivan.

_____ 4. If she doesn't **clean up her act** and start eating better, she's going to get sick.

_____ 5. Rosa was **on cloud nine** when she found out her excellent test score.

_____ 6. Vinnie asked for a **ballpark figure** on the cost of new basketball hoops for the gym.

a. taking a big risk

b. finding similarities between two totally different things

c. guess or estimate of price

d. extremely happy

e. change behavior from negative to positive

f. always buying what others have—especially the latest trends

g. rely on past achievements rather than do something new

Apply

Work with a partner to find out the meaning of each proverb. (Use an online or print dictionary.) Then work together to write a sentence for each item.

1. look out for number one

2. get cold feet

3. down in the dumps

4. put the pedal to the metal

5. at the drop of a hat

6. music to my ears

7. offer an olive branch

8. fever pitch

Vocabulary for Comprehension

Read the following passage, in which some of the words you have studied in Lessons 13–15 appear in boldface type. Then answer questions 1–6.

The Rain Forest

One **ecosystem** getting a lot of attention today is the tropical rain forest. In this unusual environment, animals, plants, and the natural setting all work together. **Photosynthesis**
5 produces huge amounts of oxygen. The trees also absorb carbon dioxide as sunlight shines on the forest canopy. Each tree produces **copious** amounts of water. This is why clouds hang over most rain forests. Clouds help **foster**
10 a moist climate that is constantly renewed.

One **benefit** of this moisture is that it helps grow plenty of plants, which animals and insects **consume**. This constant food source has allowed millions of different **species** of
15 living things to develop. As they **seek** out and

feed on each other, each species also creates a variety of ways to defend itself. Some of these defenses are chemicals that the organisms produce. Scientists use many
20 of these chemicals to produce drugs, foods, cosmetics, and medicines. As a **consequence**, the value of rain forests has increased. The search for new chemical substances has become a big business. Scientists go into the
25 rain forests to find useful products. Many of the cancer drugs recently developed came from rain forest plants. The whole world would feel the **impact** if we were ever to lose our rain forests. They make valuable contributions. We
30 would be foolish to cut them all down.

1. In line 8, **copious** means:
   - A plentiful
   - B adequate
   - C substantial
   - D minimal

2. When you **foster** (line 9) something, you:
   - A leave it behind
   - B keep it from happening
   - C help to nourish it
   - D treat it like a child

3. Another term for **consume** (line 13) is
   - A eat in great quantity
   - B let go
   - C have a conversation
   - D rest upon

4. An example of a **species** (line 14) is:
   - A requirements
   - B clouds
   - C furniture
   - D cats

5. Something that we **seek** (line 15) we:
   - A run from
   - B hide away
   - C search for
   - D travel to

6. If something is the **consequence** (line 21) of an action, it:
   - A is someone else's responsibility
   - B happens during the action
   - C is what caused the action
   - D is what happens as a result

UNIT 6 ⟪

The Best Ideas From Ancient Times

LESSON **16** **The Write Beginning**
An archaeologist studies the ancient roots of written language.

bulk	inferences	report
commenced	nevertheless	scribe
enrich	random	uniform
formal		

LESSON **17** **Citizen for a Day**
A debate explores the pros and cons of life in ancient Greece.

abnormal	dignity	mosaic
architecture	durable	normal
classic	enormous	norms
columns		

LESSON **18** **The Glory That Is Rome**
A citizen of ancient Rome shares his appreciation for Roman civilization.

abundant	doctrine	plenty
authority	downfall	premier
concept	impose	range
cornerstone		

▶ **Watch** a video introduction to this passage at **vocabularyforsuccess.com**.

Listen to this passage at **vocabularyforsuccess.com**.

Right: Dr. Denise Schmandt-Besserat's studies of ancient tokens taught us about early counting and writing.

The Write Beginning

<nonfiction narrative>

Dr. Denise Schmandt-Besserat became a researcher with a mission when she visited an ancient Mesopotamian archaeological site in the Middle East. There, she saw tiny clay objects in uniform shapes, and was fascinated. Some were shaped like miniature animals or tools; others were simple forms but had seemingly random markings. Many researchers said it was not possible to learn how these objects were used thousands of years ago. Nevertheless, Dr. Schmandt-Besserat commenced her own study of these mysterious objects, confident that she could find some answers.

Over time, Dr. Schmandt-Besserat discovered something remarkable. The clay objects had been made by the Mesopotamian society as part of a formal system that helped buyers and sellers keep track of goods. A scribe, a specially trained writer, would create these tokens out of small, moist clay tablets. Markings stood for different products, such as a bushel of grain or a jar of olive oil.

Dr. Schmandt-Besserat discovered that, at first, Mesopotamians sealed the tokens inside clay storage containers. If someone wanted to report on a container's contents, the container had to be opened. Later, Mesopotamians came up with a better idea. They used a token to make an impression on the outside of a container before they sealed the token inside. Over time, this system was further improved. People realized that a symbol could also

ᔿ VOCABULARY ᔾ

uniform	scribe
random	report
nevertheless	bulk
commenced	inferences
formal	enrich

represent a quantity and stand for a numerical amount. If a farmer was selling products in bulk, a numerical symbol was a good way to represent a particular quantity of items.

Using inferences about changes in markings and symbols, Dr. Schmandt-Besserat determined that writing grew out of the need to count. Eventually, tokens were replaced with picture symbols, which helped improve, or enrich, the nature of writing. The result was that ancient peoples began to communicate in writing, telling not only *how many*, but also *who*, *what*, *when*, *where*, and *how*. These are the same questions that Dr. Schmandt-Besserat seeks to answer every day.

TALK ABOUT IT

With a partner, answer the questions below. Use as many of the highlighted words in the selection as you can.

1. How did Dr. Schmandt-Besserat use *inferences* to understand what she uncovered?

2. In what ways do you think we *enrich* writing by adding new symbols?

Right: Mesopotamians used tokens like these to track the sale of goods.

Word Meanings

For each highlighted word on pages 176–177, the meaning is given below. For practice with other meanings, see pages 181–183. For synonyms and antonyms, see page 206.

1. uniform
(YOO-ni-form)

(adj.) Items that are *uniform* are the same in some way, such as in shape, or they are always the same and don't change.

(n.) A *uniform* is a special set of clothes worn by one group of people, such as police officers or students who go to the same school.

2. random
(RAN-duhm)

(adj.) When something is *random*, it doesn't have a plan, purpose, or pattern.

3. nevertheless
(ne-vur-thuh-LESS)

(adv.) *Nevertheless* means "in spite of" or "however." You might know that the water in a swimming pool is cold, but you jump in *nevertheless*.

4. commenced
(kuh-MENST)

(v.) An event that has *commenced* has started. If you *commenced* your research, you began it.

5. formal
(FOR-muhl)

(adj.) Something that is *formal* follows the rules set up for it.

(adj.) *Formal* events are official or proper, such as a *formal* dance.

6. scribe
(skribe)

(n.) A *scribe* is a writer, particularly one from ancient times who was specially trained to make copies of texts by hand.

7. report
(ri-PORT)

(v.) When you *report* on something, you tell about it or describe it.

(n.) A *report* gives facts and information about a subject. A report can be put in writing or given orally.

8. bulk
(buhlk)

(n.) Something that is sold in *bulk* is sold in large quantities. In some stores you can buy food in *bulk*, such as a dozen cans of beans rather than just one.

(n.) If you get the *bulk* of a person's inheritance, you get most of it.

9. inferences
(IN-fur-en-siz)

(n.) *Inferences* are good guesses, or conclusions, that you make based on facts and your own experiences.

10. enrich
(en-RICH)

(v.) When you *enrich* something, you make it richer or better. Packaged foods can be *enriched* with extra vitamins and minerals.

Word Talk

Each lesson word has been placed in a category. With a partner, discuss and list items that belong in each category. Compare your results with those of another pair of students.

Activities That You Will *Commence* Soon

Objects That Are *Uniform* in Shape

Items You Can Buy in *Bulk*

Conditions That Help You Make *Inferences* About the Weather

Objects That Move *Randomly*

Things a *Scribe* Might Copy

Things That Can *Enrich* Your Life

People to Whom You Would Send a *Formal* Letter

Activities You Dislike, Yet Do *Nevertheless*

Events *Reported* in the News

Check for Understanding

Choose the lesson word that completes each sentence. Write the word on the line provided. Some words will be used twice.

bulk	formal	report
commenced	inferences	scribe
enrich	nevertheless	uniform
	random	

1. The hikers _____ their trek at dawn and returned by sunset.

2. I saw the movie in a theater last year but watched it on TV _____.

3. The writer visited the war-torn country to _____ on the hardships of the people living there.

4. Raisins that come in small packs are costly, so I buy them in _____ to save money.

5. She ran the meeting in the _____ manner set by the rules committee.

6. My sister said she felt like an ancient _____ when she helped copy the invitations by hand.

7. The chef will _____ the soup by adding cream and spices.

8. The _____ holes that I see here and there on the tree were the work of woodpeckers.

9. All the eggs were _____, except one that was larger than the rest.

10. Part of an archeologist's work is to make _____ about a civilization based on his or her study of items the society left behind.

11. Rather than make a/an _____ speech, the mayor chatted with the voters.

12. I sent a text message to Dad to _____ the final score of the game.

Expand Word Meanings

Read the paragraph below to learn other meanings for some of the lesson words.

Jen had been working on a report on the history of written language. She needed a break, so she opened a family scrapbook. The bulk of the photos had been taken before she was born. She found a picture of her grandmother dressed for a formal occasion in a pink dress. She also found some poems that Grandma wrote as a teenager. A photo on the next page showed Granddad dressed in an army uniform. During the war, he wrote articles for magazines. Some of them were in the scrapbook. Thanks to the photos, Jen learned a lot about how important written language was to her own family.

Some of the words are used in a different way here than elsewhere in the lesson. For example, in this paragraph *report* is used as a noun that means "an account that gives facts and information." Can you figure out the meaning of the other highlighted words as they are used here? Check page 178 to confirm meanings.

Apply Other Meanings

Complete each sentence with a highlighted word from the paragraph above.

1. A police officer dressed in a blue _____ directed traffic away from the fallen tree.

2. The _____ of the players were warming up 30 minutes before the game.

3. The new club president was sworn in at a/an _____ ceremony that all members attended.

4. A/An _____ in the newspaper described the ongoing debate over raising the minimum wage.

5. When my brother worked at the grocery store, he wore a bright green _____ like all the other workers.

6. The table for the _____ dinner was set with antique silverware and cloth napkins.

7. You can read all the details of the trial in a newspaper _____ published today.

8. Each player had to try on his new _____ to see if it fit.

9. The students who helped to plant the garden were pleased that they were able to complete the _____ of their work before it got too hot outside.

10. The weather _____ on TV describes the weekend weather as warm and sunny.

LESSON 16

Word Associations

Use what you know about the lesson word in italics to answer each question. Circle the letter next to the phrase that best answers the question. Be prepared to explain your answers.

1. Which is sold in *bulk* at an office supply store?

   a. office furniture

   b. 1 computer

   c. pack of 12 pencils

2. Which word could you use instead of *nevertheless*?

   a. because

   b. however

   c. also

3. Which would be a job for a *scribe*?

   a. writing a novel

   b. copying a speech by hand

   c. typing letters

4. Which would you likely include in a *report* about an ancient empire?

   a. facts about its culture

   b. a made-up story about its kings

   c. information about your friend

5. Which worker wears a *uniform* on the job?

   a. teacher

   b. postal worker

   c. detective

6. Which event is most likely to have *commenced* after dark?

   a. nature hike

   b. family picnic

   c. fireworks display

7. What can you do to *enrich* a story?

   a. add descriptive words

   b. tell it aloud

   c. publish it in a magazine

8. Which occurs in a *random* way?

   a. lines on the highway

   b. spots on a dog

   c. stripes on a country's flag

9. Which discussion takes place in a *formal* setting?

   a. gossip

   b. a family quarrel

   c. a presidential debate

10. What can you do to make *inferences* about a person's feelings?

    a. look at the person's clothing

    b. listen to the person's tone of voice

    c. ask how the person is feeling

Check Again

Use what you know about the lesson word in italics to complete each sentence. Be sure your sentences make sense.

1. I would feel like a *scribe* if I _____

2. Before school *commenced* for the day, I _____

3. The White House is a *formal* setting because _____
   _____

4. A person's *uniform* can reveal _____

5. A *report* on the last Ice Age might include _____
   _____

6. Clouds in the sky have *random* shapes because _____
   _____

7. I wish I could spend the *bulk* of my day _____

8. The Internet is a good source of information; *nevertheless,* ___
   _____

9. To *enrich* my understanding of the past, I might visit _____

10. I can make *inferences* about a subject by _____
    _____

Challenge Yourself

Follow the directions to write sentences with the lesson words in italics. Be sure your sentences make sense both grammatically and in meaning.

1. Write a sentence with the word *report* in the seventh position.

2. Write a sentence exactly ten words in length using the word *random*.

3. Write a sentence telling what you think it would be like to work as a *scribe*.

LESSON **16**

Word-Solving Strategies:
Context Clues

Inferences

Sometimes an unfamiliar word is not defined or explained in a text. You must look for clues before or after the word to help you make an inference about a word's meaning. Read these sentences from "The Write Beginning."

> If a farmer was selling products in bulk, a numerical symbol was a good way to represent a particular quantity of items.

In this example, you can use the phrase *quantity of items* to infer that something in **bulk** is a large quantity.

Hints about a word's meaning are not always found in a sentence. Consider this sentence from "The Write Beginning":

Eventually, tokens were replaced with picture symbols, which helped improve, or enrich, the nature of writing.

There is no clue in the sentence that would help you infer the meaning of the word *tokens*. You would have to use a dictionary to learn its meaning.

BE CAREFUL!

Practice

A. Read the paragraph. In the first two boxes, write a highlighted word and an inference clue that helped you determine word meaning. Then write the meaning.

Do you have what it takes to become an archaeologist? You may be interested in the past, but are you tenacious as well as curious? Archaeologists have to spend a lot of time searching where to dig. Often, their digs find nothing. It's not a job for someone who gives up easily. Once a dig begins, archaeologists work slowly and carefully. The painstaking job of unearthing ancient objects includes endless digging, picking, and dusting. It's rewarding work, but it takes determination and patience.

WORD	INFERENCE CLUE	MEANING

B. Write a sentence for two of the highlighted words from the paragraph above. Provide inference clues.

1. _____

_____

2. _____

_____

184

Practice for Tests

Fill in the bubble next to the answer that best completes the sentence or answers the question.

1. Read this sentence.

   Sally likes to *enrich* her vocabulary by reading.

   Enrich means:
   - **A** thin out
   - **B** improve
   - **C** change
   - **D** soften

2. Another name for a *scribe* is:
   - **A** scientist
   - **B** historian
   - **C** writer
   - **D** anthropologist

3. Northerners know winter has *commenced* when:
   - **A** the wind blows
   - **B** the first flowers bloom
   - **C** the leaves turn red
   - **D** snow falls

4. Something is *random* if it:
   - **A** is done deliberately
   - **B** doesn't have a pattern
   - **C** has a set purpose
   - **D** always moves in the same way

5. The opposite of *formal* is:
   - **A** proper
   - **B** clear
   - **C** casual
   - **D** official

6. Read this sentence.

   I run every day; *nevertheless,* the cross-country race was difficult.

   Nevertheless means:
   - **A** at no time
   - **B** except
   - **C** likewise
   - **D** despite that

7. Items are *uniform* if they are:
   - **A** oddly shaped
   - **B** worn by one group of people
   - **C** the same size and shape
   - **D** unbalanced

8. A person buying in *bulk* would NOT:
   - **A** save money
   - **B** buy individual items
   - **C** buy in large quantities
   - **D** have a lot to put away

9. A word closely related to *inferences* is:
   - **A** conclusions
   - **B** knowledge
   - **C** certainties
   - **D** consequences

10. A good television news *report* should:
    - **A** entertain people of all ages
    - **B** focus on issues for debate
    - **C** give clear and factual information
    - **D** present local events

Watch a video introduction to this passage at **vocabularyforsuccess.com**.

Listen to this passage at **vocabularyforsuccess.com**.

Citizen for a Day

<debate>

Today's debate question is: *Would you like to have lived in ancient Greece?*

Jacob: Yes, I would like to have lived in ancient Greece. What normal person would *not* love to have lived there? It was one of the world's most remarkable civilizations. I will give two reasons to support my view.

Ancient Greece had magnificent architecture. The Greeks built enormous temples and other public buildings that were so durable that many, like the Parthenon, are still standing today. Thanks to their elegant columns and beautiful decorations in mosaic, it's no wonder that people still copy the ideas of classic Greek style. Second, and more importantly, ancient Greece was the birthplace of democracy. In fact, the word *democracy* comes from the Greek language. Elections, laws, representative government, and human rights are just some of the ideas we owe to the Greeks. I can't think of a more exciting place to have been a citizen.

Keisha: I think I speak for all female students when I say I would *not* have liked living in ancient Greece. Why? The ancient Greeks' view of democracy was different from ours. Legal rights and human rights did not apply to all people—especially not to women! In ancient Greece, women had no rights and could not vote. While the norms for men

VOCABULARY

normal	mosaic
architecture	classic
enormous	norms
durable	abnormal
columns	dignity

included fighting battles, making speeches, and going to the theater, women could not even leave their homes without permission. To me, that is not fair. That kind of life is abnormal. In fact, in Greece rights of any kind were reserved for only about one-eighth of the population. If you weren't born to the right parents or were an immigrant, you had no rights at all.

Finally, Jacob neglected to mention another fact of ancient Greek life. Almost *one-third* of all people in Greece were enslaved. Slaves had no rights. They lived and died building Greece and its great buildings. Ancient Greece did not believe in the dignity of *all* men and women—just that of a select few. That's why I certainly would not have wanted to live there!

TALK ABOUT IT

With a partner, answer the questions below. Use as many of the highlighted words in the selection as you can.

1. Do you think Keisha's views are *normal* or *abnormal*? Why? What about Jacob's views?

2. How would you compare the *norms* of life in ancient Greece with the norms of life today?

Word Meanings

vocabularyforsuccess.com

▶ **Watch** a video introduction for each word

◀)) **Listen** to iWords🎵

📖 **Refer** to the online dictionary

For each highlighted word on pages 186–187, the meaning is given below. For practice with other meanings, turn to pages 191–193. For synonyms and antonyms, see page 206.

1. normal
(NOR-muhl)

(adj.) Something that is *normal* is regular or usual. It follows the rules.

2. architecture
(AR-ki-tek-tchur)

(n.) *Architecture* is the work of designing and constructing buildings. It is means a style of building, such as Greek *architecture*.

(n.) The way that something is designed or put together is its *architecture*. For example, the *architecture* of government is its structure.

3. enormous
(ee-NOR-muhss)

(adj.) *Enormous* objects are very large or huge. Something can be *enormous* in size or number.

4. durable
(DUR-uh-buhl)

(adj.) *Durable* items or ideas last for a long time because they are tough, strong, or sturdy.

5. columns
(KOL-uhmz)

(n.) *Columns* are stone or wooden posts. *Columns* often support a building.

(n.) A page of text might be divided into long sections called *columns*.

6. mosaic
(moh-ZAY-ik)

(n.) A *mosaic* is a picture or design made by putting together small pieces of colored material, such as glass, stone, or tile.

(n.) A *mosaic* also refers to a whole made up of smaller pieces. A journal might be called a *mosaic* of your thoughts and experiences.

7. classic
(KLA-sik)

(adj.) *Classic* ideas and objects are from or connected to ancient Greece or Rome.

(n.) A *classic* is an excellent work of art or literature that has been looked at, performed, read, or studied for years.

8. norms
(normz)

(n.) *Norms* are behaviors that people accept and follow. The *norms* for communicating have changed, and today more youths text than call.

9. abnormal
(ab-NOR-muhl)

(adj.) *Abnormal* circumstances are unusual circumstances.

10. dignity
(DIG-nuh-tee)

(n.) *Dignity* is a feeling of honor, elegance, and worthiness. If you have *dignity*, you act in a way that shows you have self-respect.

Word Talk

Each lesson word is listed here. With a partner, take turns drawing a picture to illustrate the meaning of six of the words. As one partner draws, the other partner identifies the vocabulary word.

abnormal

architecture

classic (adj.)

columns

dignity

durable

enormous

mosaic

normal

norms

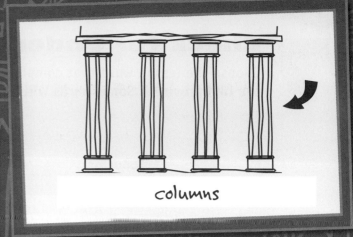

columns

Check for Understanding

Choose the lesson word that completes each sentence. Write the word on the line provided. Some words will be used twice.

abnormal	columns	mosaic
architecture	dignity	normal
classic	durable	norms
	enormous	

1. Even in modern suburbs, you can see features of _____ design.

2. Large _____ on the porch support the upper floor of the old southern home.

3. One of the _____ of summer is seeing volleyball players practice on the beach.

4. Surfers in Hawaii ride _____ waves that can be more than thirty feet high.

5. The artist will use small pieces of glass cut in uniform shapes to create the _____ that will decorate the entry hall.

6. The gnarled and twisted tree seems to have grown in a/an _____ way.

7. The modern _____ of large cities includes many huge, beautiful buildings that seem to touch the sky.

8. Tall marble _____ are all that are left of many ancient ruins.

9. My mountain bike is _____, so I can ride it on even the roughest trails.

10. The veterans marched with _____ during the parade, holding their heads high and their shoulders straight.

11. It is unusually dry this year, but in _____ years we get plenty of rain.

12. Tourists in Rome visit _____ buildings such as the Colosseum.

Expand Word Meanings

Read the paragraph below to learn other meanings for some of the lesson words.

The Agora of ancient Athens was a marketplace as well as a gathering place. Unlike today, not all citizens were welcome to participate in public life in Greece. Women were seldom seen at the Agora. Still, it was a mosaic of Greek culture and the center of public life. There you might talk to an artist or see a politician who helped create the architecture of democracy. You would see slaves, merchants, and traders. You might discuss the performance of a play that is now a Greek classic. You could also hear important issues debated publicly. We read about similar topics and scenes in the pages and columns of newspapers today.

> **!** Some of the words in this lesson are used here in a different way. For example, the noun *mosaic* on this page means "a whole made up of smaller pieces." Can you figure out the meaning of the other highlighted words as they are used here? Refer to page 188 to confirm meanings.

Apply Other Meanings

Complete each sentence with a highlighted word from the paragraph above.

1. The tunes from all the band's instruments came together to form a/an _____ of sounds that thrilled the audience.

2. The homeowner studied many garden-design books before deciding on the _____ of his new garden.

3. I searched the online library catalog to find an American _____ to read this month.

4. The entries in the dictionary appear in two _____ on each page.

5. The author admitted that the main character in his novel is a/an _____ of real people he has known.

6. I skimmed the _____ of the magazine's pages, looking for celebrity news.

7. The class performed a scene from *Romeo and Juliet,* then discussed the _____.

8. The _____ of the new school curriculum allows young children plenty of time for free play.

9. There were two _____ of questions to answer on the multiple-choice test.

10. Many people say this science fiction book is a timeless _____, but I don't agree.

Word Associations

Use what you know about the lesson word in italics to answer each question. Circle the letter next to the phrase that best answers the question. Be prepared to explain your answers.

1. Which of these is best described as *enormous?*

   a. passenger car

   b. oil tanker

   c. model train

2. Which material could be used to create a *mosaic*?

   a. a can of paint

   b. large blocks of wood

   c. small pieces of tile

3. Which best describes a *classic* piece of literature?

   a. enjoyed for many years

   b. a popular new book

   c. published every week

4. For which worker is traveling during work hours part of a *normal* workday?

   a. homemaker

   b. airline mechanic

   c. flight attendant

5. Which does NOT describe the purpose of *columns*?

   a. to support

   b. to decorate

   c. to provide entry

6. Which structure is most closely linked to the *architecture* of a large city?

   a. single-family home

   b. high-rise apartment building

   c. gas station

7. Which behavior is *abnormal* in pets such as cats and dogs?

   a. scratching now and then

   b. daytime napping

   c. constant licking

8. Which person is expected to show *dignity* on the job?

   a. president

   b. actor

   c. hockey player

9. Which footwear might be described as especially *durable?*

   a. sneakers

   b. hiking boots

   c. sandals

10. Which is one of the *norms* for all students?

    a. doing homework

    b. riding a bus

    c. playing sports

Check Again

Use what you know about the lesson word in italics to complete each sentence. Be sure your sentences make sense.

1. It's important for textbooks to be *durable* because _____

_____

2. One of the *norms* for car drivers is _____

3. If I were creating a *mosaic*, I would use _____

4. In an emergency such as a fire, a *normal* person would _____

_____

5. The *architecture* of our government divides power_____

_____

6. A person with *abnormal* chest pain should _____

7. I would describe a movie as *classic* if it _____

8. Three animals that can be described as *enormous* are _____

9. To read numbers or text in *columns*, you must _____

_____

10. When I act with dignity, I _____

_____

Challenge Yourself

Follow the directions to write sentences with the lesson words in italics. Be sure your sentences make sense both grammatically and in meaning.

1. Write a sentence with the word *normal* in the second position.

2. Write a sentence exactly ten words in length using the word *durable*.

3. Write a sentence telling about a work of *architecture* you would like to see one day.

Word-Solving Strategies: Roots

The root norma: "rule, pattern"

Words are often made up of different parts, such as base words and affixes such as prefixes and suffixes. However, the word part that gives a word its basic meaning is called its root.

There are many Latin roots in English words. The root *norma* is one example. *Norma* means "rule or pattern." You can use the meaning of the root *norma* to help you figure out words with the base word *norm*.

Let's examine the word *norms* from this lesson. Using the meaning of the root, you can figure out that norms are rules or patterns. They are behaviors that people accept and follow.

Now let's examine the word *normal* from this lesson. You know that *norma* means "rule or pattern," and you may also know that the suffix -*al* means "relating to or characterized

by." Using the meaning of the Latin root and the suffix, you can figure out that something *normal* is characterized by rules or patterns. In other words, things that are *normal* are regular, usual, and follow the rules.

Examples

Look at these other examples and think about how the root *norma* gives each words its basic meaning. It might help you to know that the prefix *e-* comes from the Latin *ex-*, which means "out of." The prefix *ab-* can mean "away from."

norma → norm → enormous

norma → norm → abnormal

BE CAREFUL!

Combining the meaning of a Latin root with the meaning of a prefix or suffix is a good way to start to define a word. However, if you are unsure of a word, it's always best to check a dictionary. Many words have meanings that you may not be able to figure out by just combining the meanings of roots and affixes.

Practice

Find the base word *norm* in these examples. Then use what you know about the *root* norma to figure out word meanings. Check the meanings in the dictionary.

1. abnormality _____

_____

2. normalize _____

_____

3. subnormal _____

_____

4. paranormal _____

_____

Practice for Tests

Fill in the bubble next to the answer that best completes the sentence or answers the question.

1. China is an *enormous* country that covers more than 3 million square miles.

   Enormous means:
   - ○ **A** large
   - ○ **B** superlative
   - ○ **C** huge
   - ○ **D** global

2. Someone studying *architecture* would:
   - ○ **A** learn to design buildings
   - ○ **B** work in construction
   - ○ **C** live in a large city
   - ○ **D** visit temples in Greece

3. An item of clothing is *classic* when it:
   - ○ **A** is sold in many stores
   - ○ **B** doesn't go out of style
   - ○ **C** comes in many colors
   - ○ **D** is fashionable for a few seasons

4. In which group could all the items be used in making a *mosaic*?
   - ○ **A** small shells, rocks, nuts
   - ○ **B** logs, glass cubes, pebbles
   - ○ **C** floor tiles, bricks, paint
   - ○ **D** pebbles, glass cubes, tile pieces

5. A *normal* school week would:
   - ○ **A** end on Saturday
   - ○ **B** begin on Monday
   - ○ **C** last seven days
   - ○ **D** include a holiday

6. The car's tires are made of a *durable* material that isn't damaged by rough roads.

   Durable means:
   - ○ **A** sturdy
   - ○ **B** adequate
   - ○ **C** expandable
   - ○ **D** risky

7. One of the *norms* for a sports team is to:
   - ○ **A** play weekly games
   - ○ **B** practice regularly
   - ○ **C** buy new uniforms yearly
   - ○ **D** have many fans

8. Someone with *dignity* does NOT:
   - ○ **A** listen to others
   - ○ **B** show self-respect
   - ○ **C** disrespect others
   - ○ **D** have pride

9. A word closely associated with *abnormal* is:
   - ○ **A** haphazard
   - ○ **B** identical
   - ○ **C** nuisance
   - ○ **D** unusual

10. You would most likely find *columns* in:
    - ○ **A** a newspaper
    - ○ **B** a novel
    - ○ **C** a comic book
    - ○ **D** an email

LESSON 18

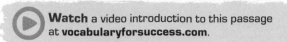 **Watch** a video introduction to this passage at **vocabularyforsuccess.com**.

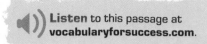 **Listen** to this passage at **vocabularyforsuccess.com**.

The Glory That Is Rome

\<speech\>

Friends, Romans, and Countrymen,

I have come before you to speak of the glory of our beloved republic.

As many of you know, as a citizen and an elected leader of the Roman republic, I have abundant authority to discuss this important topic. I come from a well-known Roman family that believes in helping to improve our society. Even as a boy, I looked forward to a career in government. To prepare for my future, I studied Latin, Greek, philosophy, public speaking, and a range of other subjects. My education gave me the rich background needed for the work I do today.

I have devoted my life to Rome. When I was a young man, I proudly served in the Roman army. Later, I became a laywer, and after that, a judge. As a censor, I conducted the census to count all the citizens in Rome. To pay for our beautiful buildings and art, I voted to impose taxes on our citizens. It was not a popular decision, but it was the right one. Now I am a senator, just as my father and grandfather were. Every day I have plenty of opportunities to aid the citizens of Rome. It is an honor to have a job that allows me to help others.

We Romans are fortunate to enjoy the most important, in fact, the premier, government in the entire world. After all, we offer citizenship to many people. Sometimes we even extend the concept of citizenship to those we have conquered. Our doctrine of citizenship gives people rights and protections by law. Indeed, our system of laws is the cornerstone of our republic. As senators, we vote on important issues and create new laws to help our people. This is hard work. We do not always agree. But we cannot ignore our laws or the needs of our citizens. That would lead to Rome's downfall. Therefore, let us proudly join together to work for Rome, our glorious republic.

Left: A bust of the Cicero, a Roman philosopher, lawyer, and statesman.

Below: In this scene from a film about ancient Rome, a politician gives a speech in the Senate.

VOCABULARY

abundant	premier
authority	concept
range	doctrine
impose	cornerstone
plenty	downfall

TALK ABOUT IT

With a partner, answer the questions below. Use as many of the highlighted words in the selection as you can.

1. Why does the speaker say he has *abundant authority* to talk about Rome?

2. Why do you think the speaker feels that Rome is the world's *premier* government?

Word Meanings

vocabularyforsuccess.com

▶ **Watch** a video introduction for each word

◀)) **Listen** to iWords

📖 **Refer** to the online dictionary

For each highlighted word on pages 196–197, the meaning is given below. For practice with other meanings, turn to pages 201–203. For synonyms and antonyms, see page 206.

1. abundant
(uh-BUN-duhnt)

(adj.) If something is *abundant*, there is a large amount of it or more than enough. There is *abundant* sunshine in the desert.

2. authority
(uh-THOR-uh-tee)

(n.) If you have *authority*, you have the right or power to do something. Similarly, a person in power is called an *authority*.

(n.) Someone who knows a great deal about a subject is an *authority* on it. A farmer is an *authority* on cultivating crops.

3. range
(raynj)

(n.) A *range* is a variety or series of things. If you play a *range* of sports, you might play volleyball, soccer, and tennis.

(v.) Something can *range*, or change or vary, within limits. The temperature might *range* from 68 to 72 degrees Fahrenheit.

4. impose
(im-POZE)

(v.) When you *impose* something, you force it upon others. A government can *impose* taxes. Parents might *impose* curfews on teenagers.

5. plenty
(PLEN-tee)

(n.) *Plenty* is an amount that is enough or more than enough. You might be given *plenty* of homework today or have *plenty* of time to play this weekend.

6. premier
(pri-MIHR)

(adj.) Something is called *premier* if it is best, first, or most important.

(n.) *Premier* is a title given to some countries' political leader. China has a *premier* who is the head of government.

7. concept
(KON-sept)

(n.) A *concept* is a thought or a general idea of what something is like. Your *concept* of what's fun may be different from your friend's idea of a good time.

8. doctrine
(DOK-trin)

(n.) A *doctrine* is a teaching, belief, or policy of a group or a government. Many world leaders have supported a doctrine of human rights.

9. cornerstone
(KOR-nur-stone)

(n.) A *cornerstone* is the foundation of something. Democracy is the *cornerstone* of our government.

(n.) A *cornerstone* is also a stone that joins two walls of a building at a corner. Printed on a *cornerstone* might be a date or information about the building.

10. downfall
(DOUN-fawl)

(n.) A *downfall* is a sudden fall from power or a decline in importance. Historians often discuss the *downfall* of ancient Rome.

Word Talk

Each lesson word has been placed in a category. With a partner, discuss and list items that belong in each category. Compare your results with those of another pair of students.

People Who Have *Authority* in School	*Premier* Vacation Spots

Things That Are *Abundant* in Nature	Examples from the *Range* of Snow Activities	People Who Are Considered a *Cornerstone* of the United States	People or Groups That Have *Doctrines*

Popular *Concepts* for Science Fiction Movies	People Who Might *Impose* a Penalty	Things That Can Cause a Leader's *Downfall*	Places That Have *Plenty* of Space

Check for Understanding

Choose the lesson word that completes each sentence. Write the word on the line provided. Some words will be used twice.

abundant	cornerstone	plenty
authority	doctrine	premier
concept	downfall	range
	impose	

1. The _____ restaurant in town has excellent food and an award-winning chef.

2. A/An _____ of peace can be found in the teachings of many great people.

3. _____ rains ended the year-long drought and drenched the farmlands.

4. The students' hard work was the _____ of the successful fundraiser.

5. I'm set in my ways, so my friends don't try to _____ their ideas on me.

6. The team's _____ came when its star player was injured on the field.

7. The _____ of artists at the fair included painters, potters, and weavers.

8. A healthy diet includes lots of whole grains and _____ of vegetables.

9. I think the _____ of kindness should include caring for animals as well as for people.

10. Because they have _____ wealth, the family gives to many charities.

11. The President has the _____ to veto bills passed by Congress.

12. A neighborhood night patrol led to the _____ of the local car thieves.

Expand Word Meanings

Read the paragraph below to learn other meanings for some of the lesson words.

Sam read the cornerstone of the ancient Greek building, which was dedicated to the people, and thought about democracy. Democracy has lasted a long time. Today, countries that practice democracy range from the United States and Canada to Switzerland, India, and many others around the globe. The head of a country, such as a president or a premier, might lead a democracy. But the citizens have a say in running it, too. This was the ancient Greek ideal. Each citizen is an authority on his or her own needs. In a democracy, they can vote to support their causes. They can also protest to change laws.

> Some of the words in this lesson are used here in a different way. For example, the noun *cornerstone* is used here to mean "a stone that joins two walls of a building at a corner." Can you figure out the meaning of the other highlighted words as they are used here? Refer to page 198 to confirm meanings.

Apply Other Meanings

Complete each sentence with a highlighted word from the paragraph above.

1. My grandmother has spent a lot of time in Mexico, Costa Rica, and Brazil and is a/an _____ on Latin American culture.

2. The date on which the new school opened was carved on its _____.

3. Depending on the season, I enjoy sports that _____ from soccer to swimming.

4. On a visit to Ottawa, the students listened to the _____ and other Canadian politicians speak about issues that concern young people.

5. The cost of a hardcover book may _____ from a few dollars to more than twenty dollars.

6. The builder chose a special piece of marble for the _____ of the new government building.

7. When Dad had a question about taxes, he went to his accountant who is a/an _____ on income tax laws.

8. The colors of a tabby cat can _____ from orange to gray to brown.

9. I told my brother to stop bossing me around as if he's the _____ of our family.

10. If the _____ is not set properly, the entire building will appear to be crooked.

Word Associations

LESSON 18

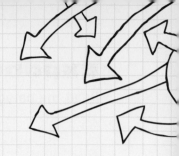

Use what you know about the lesson word in italics to answer each question. Circle the letter next to the phrase that best answers the question. Be prepared to explain your answers.

1. Which person is NOT an *authority* on medicine?

   a. patient
   b. doctor
   c. pharmacist

2. Which shows a *range* of temperatures?

   a. "It will be hot today and tomorrow."
   b. "The weatherman said it will 70 to 80 degrees tomorrow."
   c. "At noon it will 70 degrees outside."

3. Which structure has a *cornerstone*?

   a. rock wall
   b. patio
   c. building

4. Which is something a coach might *impose*?

   a. a new gym
   b. extra practice
   c. players on the team

5. Which place offers *abundant* fruits and vegetables?

   a. florist
   b. farmers' market
   c. candy shop

6. Which individual's *concept* of a typical school day is different from yours?

   a. preschooler
   b. best friend
   c. seventh-grade student

7. Which person might greet a *premier* visiting from another country?

   a. tourist
   b. student
   c. president

8. Which vehicle has *plenty* of room for many passengers?

   a. motorcycle
   b. limousine
   c. compact car

9. Which might cause the *downfall* of a company?

   a. long hours
   b. poor sales
   c. effective advertisements

10. Which person might speak about *doctrines*?

   a. chef
   b. athlete
   c. politician

Check Again

Use what you know about the lesson word in italics to complete each sentence. Be sure your sentences make sense.

1. If a car has *plenty* of gas, it will _____

2. A person of *authority* whom I respect is _____

3. If there is *abundant* snowfall, _____

4. Education is the *cornerstone* of _____

5. One hardship that a flood might *impose* on its victims is _____
_____

6. The *range* of students' ages in the class in the next room is probably _____

7. A foreign *premier* visiting this country might enjoy _____
_____

8. The *downfall* of some famous people is _____
_____

9. If I could speak to all Americans, I would share a *doctrine* of _____
_____

10. My *concept* for a better car is _____
_____

Challenge Yourself

Write Your Own

Follow the directions to write sentences with the lesson words in italics. Be sure your sentences make sense both grammatically and in meaning.

1. Write a sentence with the word *authority* in the fourth position.

2. Write a sentence exactly ten words in length using the word *range*.

3. Write a sentence describing your thoughts about college life using the word *concept*.

Word-Solving Strategies: Context Clues

Synonyms

Sometimes an author will give you a clue about an unfamiliar word by using a synonym in the text. Here is an example:

> We Romans are fortunate to enjoy the most important, in fact, the premier, government in the entire world.

Look for synonyms before or after a word. Notice that in this sentence from "The Glory That Is Rome," the synonym *most important* comes before the lesson word **premier**.

A synonym for an unfamiliar word may not appear in the same sentence.

> *We can learn from the downfall of Rome. Its failure can teach us many lessons.*

In the example above, the synonym for *downfall—failure—*is in the next sentence. Be sure to look in nearby sentences for synonyms.

BE CAREFUL!

Practice

A. Read the paragraph. Write each highlighted word and its synonym in the first two boxes. Then write a meaning for the word in the third box.

"Friends and fellow classmates," Jamil began in an anxious voice. He loathed giving speeches in school. The only thing he hated more was a long car trip with his little brother. There had to be some way to make this ordeal less of a hardship. Jamil closed his eyes for a second and imagined that he was a famous Roman orator—a speaker everyone in the Forum wanted to hear. Then he held his arms wide and spoke with confidence.

WORD	SYNONYM	WORD MEANING

B. Write a sentence for each of the highlighted words from the paragraph above. Use a synonym as a context clue. You will use one word twice.

1. _____

2. _____

3. _____

4. _____

Practice for Tests

Fill in the bubble next to the answer that best completes the sentence or answers the question.

1. Read this sentence.

   The *cornerstone* of dignity is self-respect.

   Cornerstone means:

   ○ **A** consequence
   ○ **B** hardship
   ○ **C** foundation
   ○ **D** challenge

2. A word associated with *doctrine* is:
   ○ **A** belief
   ○ **B** explanation
   ○ **C** document
   ○ **D** hypothesis

3. Two qualities of an *authority* are:
   ○ **A** interest and intelligence
   ○ **B** knowledge and experience
   ○ **C** boldness and friendliness
   ○ **D** kindness and generosity

4. A person with *plenty* of opinions:
   ○ **A** is always amusing to talk to
   ○ **B** would always be wrong
   ○ **C** could be a biased person
   ○ **D** would get along with everyone

5. The opposite of *abundant* is:
   ○ **A** limited
   ○ **B** numerous
   ○ **C** generous
   ○ **D** weak

6. Read this sentence.

   My *concept* of good entertainment is a movie that keeps me guessing.

   Concept means:

   ○ **A** complaint
   ○ **B** idea
   ○ **C** criticism
   ○ **D** source

7. When you *impose* something, you do NOT:
   ○ **A** force it upon others
   ○ **B** insist upon it
   ○ **C** give others a choice
   ○ **D** set it up without discussion

8. A *premier* works for:
   ○ **A** a movie company
   ○ **B** a corporation
   ○ **C** a charity
   ○ **D** a government

9. An essay on the *downfall* of a nation:
   ○ **A** discusses how it became less powerful
   ○ **B** describes its architecture
   ○ **C** tells about its military successes
   ○ **D** celebrates the nation's culture

10. A wide *range* of classes might include:
    ○ **A** a new math class
    ○ **B** math and science
    ○ **C** music three times a week
    ○ **D** music, art, science, math

Synonyms and Antonyms

In the following Word Bank, you will find synonyms and antonyms for some of the words in Lessons 16–18. (Remember: Some words have both synonyms and antonyms.) Study these words; then complete the exercises below.

together	ended	temporary	customs	force	wealth
mention	scarce	hide	valuable	huge	varied

A. For each sentence, fill in the blank with a SYNONYM for the word in boldface.

1. Although Lily was familiar with the **norms** of the Chinese New Year celebration, her best friend, Sarah, didn't know any of the _____ .

2. A/An _____ avalanche buried an **enormous** lake under fifty feet of rocks and mud, completely erasing it from the landscape.

3. The club secretary was asked to **report** the highlights from the last meeting. Did he _____ how many people were able to attend?

4. The reef contained a/an _____ of fish because there were **plenty** of hiding spaces and food.

5. My little brother tried to **impose** his will upon on our family by trying to _____ everyone do what he wanted in order to keep him from screaming at the top of his lungs.

B. For each sentence, fill in the blank with an ANTONYM for the word in boldface.

6. In cold climates, you need a **durable** shelter, not a/an _____ , flimsy shack.

7. Good citizens **report** suspicious activities while criminals _____ information about their wrongdoing.

8. Even though grass provided an **abundant** source of food, larger animals were _____ because of a lack of available water.

9. The graduation ceremony **commenced** with the students filing quietly into the auditorium and _____ with them cheering and applauding.

10. A machine in a factory produces **uniform** pieces, while something that is handcrafted by artists can be _____ in shape or form.

Word Study: Proverbs

If team members cannot agree and constantly argue, you may say the team will soon fail. The word downfall (Lesson 18) expresses this same idea. So does the sentence "A house divided cannot stand." This expression is an example of a proverb, which is a brief saying that illustrates a truth or common knowledge.

Proverbs are often described as words to live by because they give advice for how people should live their lives. For example, "Strike while the iron is hot" is a proverb that suggests taking the opportunity to take action when you can.

Practice

Read each sentence. Use context clues to figure out the meaning of each proverb in boldface. Then, write the letter of the definition for the proverb.

_____ 1. As Ben stared out the window to watch for his cousin to arrive, his sister told him, "**A watched pot never boils.**"

_____ 2. Anika's parents told her she couldn't stay alone in the house because **when the cat's away, the mice will play.**

_____ 3. When you're tempted to play video games all day, remember **variety is the spice of life.**

_____ 4. When Regina complained that she wished she had more money, her mother told her that **if wishes were horses then beggars would ride.**

_____ 5. Carrie said she smiles at everyone she sees because **kindness begets kindness.**

_____ 6. When I asked Lee for a favor, he said, "**I'll scratch your back if you'll scratch mine.**

a. if you're nice to people, they will be nice to you

b. I'll do something for you if you do something for me

c. if you want something, you have to act

d. what you deserve to get is never far away

e. waiting anxiously for something makes the time seem to go more slowly

f. life is more interesting if you do many different activities

g. when there is no one to supervise, people will misbehave

Apply

Work with a partner to find out the meaning of each proverb. (Use an online or print dictionary.) Then work together to write a sentence for each item.

1. Better safe than sorry.

2. Never say die.

3. No man is an island.

4. No pain, no gain.

5. One good turn deserves another.

6. Once bitten, twice shy.

7. One rotten apple spoils the barrel.

8. Still waters run deep.

Vocabulary for Comprehension

Read the following passage, in which some of the words you have studied in Lessons 16–18 appear in boldface type. Then answer questions 1–6.

The Colosseum of Rome

Picture an **enormous** amphitheater filled with people. In the center of the huge arena, men take part in battles that **range** from hand-to-hand fighting to fierce struggles with wild
5 animals. People in the crowd cheer wildly and signal whether a fighter should live or die. It is the Colosseum of Rome. It is the **premier** spot for Roman entertainment.

Construction of the Roman Colosseum
10 **commenced** between CE 70 and CE 72. It could hold as many as 50,000 people when it was finished. Built with three tiers that provided **abundant** seating on each level, the Colosseum had about 80 entrances for spectators.

15 Documents **report** that rooms beneath the wooden floor of the Colosseum were used to hold wild animals and other items needed for the shows going on above.

The **architecture** of the Colosseum is
20 famous. Its arches and its three kinds of decorative **columns** made it grand and **durable**. But this sturdy stone-and-concrete structure would suffer over time. Eventually the Colosseum would be badly damaged by
25 lightning, earthquakes, pollution, and people. **Nevertheless,** it remains standing today as a monument to ancient Rome.

1. A product described as **premier** (line 7) is
   - ⃝ **A** just beginning
   - ⃝ **B** very expensive
   - ⃝ **C** the best of its kind
   - ⃝ **D** used for recreation

2. If a race **commenced** (line 10), it
   - ⃝ **A** ended
   - ⃝ **B** lasted
   - ⃝ **C** was made public
   - ⃝ **D** began

3. If seating is **abundant** (line 13),
   - ⃝ **A** seating is limited
   - ⃝ **B** there are a lot of seats
   - ⃝ **C** the seats are very large
   - ⃝ **D** the seating is uncomfortable

4. The word **architecture** (line 19) means
   - ⃝ **A** building style
   - ⃝ **B** building materials
   - ⃝ **C** person who designs buildings
   - ⃝ **D** foundation

5. A **durable** object (line 22) is NOT
   - ⃝ **A** strong
   - ⃝ **B** long-lasting
   - ⃝ **C** poorly made
   - ⃝ **D** well-built

6. Another meaning for **nevertheless** (line 26) is
   - ⃝ **A** likewise
   - ⃝ **B** such as
   - ⃝ **C** meanwhile
   - ⃝ **D** however

DISAPPEARED!

LESSON 19

The Mystery of the Minoans

How could this ancient civilization disappear without a trace?

appalled	credible	reside
appeal	prey	theory
appear	region	variable
appropriate		

LESSON 20

The Anasazi People

What made the Anasazi people desert their cliff dwellings?

ally	cease	incredible
apparatus	disperse	pare
assault	feature	robust
brink		

LESSON 21

The Easter Island Puzzle

Why did an ancient people build these extraordinary statues?

bizarre	implicate	premise
decode	leisure	reference
dramatic	motive	ritual
duplicate		

▶ **Watch** a video introduction to this passage at **vocabularyforsuccess.com**.

🔊 **Listen** to this passage at **vocabularyforsuccess.com**.

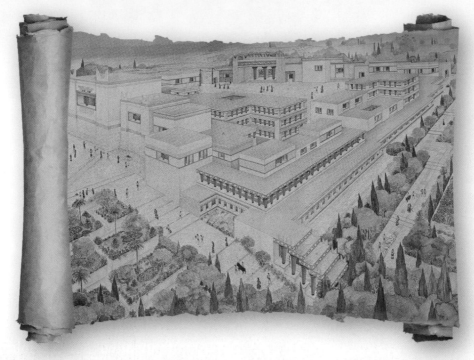

This is what archaeologists believe the Palace of Knossos area looked like.

The Mystery of the Minoans

<mystery>

Jaws must have dropped when people first stumbled upon the ruins of a temple on the Greek island of Crete. The enormous pillars and grand scale indicated *what* this structure was. However, *who* built it and *why* the builders disappeared without a trace became two of the world's greatest mysteries. Good detective work helped solve the first question. The temple had been built 5,000 years before by the Minoans, an extremely advanced society. However, for many years the second question—what happened to these people—seemed impossible to answer.

The possibilities were so variable, one possible answer after another was offered. Could enemy armies have destroyed the Minoans? At first, that seemed a credible theory. Then, many were appalled when new evidence suggested something even worse. Perhaps an enormous volcanic eruption struck the region in ancient times. Yet, if the Minoans had fallen prey to a volcanic eruption, why hadn't researchers found the skeletons of those who had died? Despite the appeal of this theory, it would appear that the eruption had occurred too recently for this to be the answer.

Scientists scrambled for new clues. Soil from the middle of the island revealed microscopic organisms that reside in the ocean. Samples of bone and pottery found near the shore had originated inland. There was only one appropriate explanation for these surprising discoveries. A tsunami must have swept across Crete, carrying away everything in its wake. However, scientists pointed out that tsunami waves occur immediately after volcanic eruptions. Thus, a tsunami couldn't be the sole answer, either.

Today, scientists believe that a volcanic eruption and floods did cause some Minoan deaths. Then, as the climate began to change as a result of the eruption, crops failed. The result was that foreign armies were able to invade and take over a weak and hungry people. While we may never know for sure what actually happened to the Minoans, scientific detectives will continue investigating this mystery.

TALK ABOUT IT

With a partner, answer the questions below. Use as many of the highlighted words in the selection as you can.

1. What is your opinion of each *theory* about the mystery of the Minoans?

2. Can you think of any other theories about their disappearance that might be *credible?*

The Royal Minoan Palace as seen today.

Word Meanings

For each highlighted word on pages 210–211, the meaning is given below. For practice with other meanings, see pages 215–217. For synonyms and antonyms, see page 240.

Watch a video introduction for each word
Listen to iWords
Refer to the online dictionary

1. **variable**
   (VAIR-ee-uh-buhl)

   (adj.) If the weather is *variable,* it is likely to change.

   (n.) A *variable* is an amount whose value is not known. In math, a *variable* is represented by a symbol like *x* or *y,* which stands for a number.

2. **credible**
   (KRED-uh-buhl)

   (adj.) A story or an explanation that is *credible* is believable.

3. **theory**
   (THIHR-ee)

   (n.) A *theory* proposes a reasonable explanation or guess based on a set of facts.

4. **appalled**
   (uh-PAWLD)

   (adj.) If you are shocked or put off by someone's bad behavior, you are *appalled* by it.

5. **region**
   (REE-juhn)

   (n.) A *region* is a large geographic area with similar land or water features, such as a mountain *region* or a lake *region.*

6. **prey**
   (pray)

   (n.) If you fall *prey* to misfortune or an attack, you are unable to resist or fight back.

7. **appeal**
   (uh-PEEL)

   (n.) If something has *appeal,* it is attractive to people and they like it or are interested in it.

   (v.) If you *appeal* to someone for help, you make an earnest request to that person for assistance.

8. **appear**
   (uh-PIHR)

   (v.) When things *appear* to be disorganized, they seem to be out of place.

   (v.) When the clouds *appear* in the sky, they come into view.

9. **reside**
   (ri-ZIDE)

   (v.) You *reside,* or live in, your home.

10. **appropriate**
    adj. (uh-PROH-pree-uht)
    v. (uh-PROH-pree-ayt)

    (adj.) Something that is correct and proper is *appropriate.* When your clothing is the right thing to wear to an event, you are wearing *appropriate* clothes.

    (v.) When you take something without permission, you *appropriate* it. If an author were to *appropriate* another author's work without giving credit, he would lose his reputation and might get sued.

Word Talk

Each lesson word has been placed in a category. With a partner, discuss and list items that belong in each category. Compare your results with those of another pair of students.

Sources That Are *Credible*	Books That Have *Appeal*

Places Where People *Reside*	Misfortunes People Are *Prey* To	Ways to *Appear* to Be Concerned	Things That Might Be *Variable*

Cold *Regions* of the Earth	Things You Might Have a *Theory* About	*Appropriate* Ways to Communicate with Your Friends	Things That *Appall* You

Check for Understanding

Choose the lesson word that completes each sentence. Write the word on the line provided. Some words will be used twice.

appalled	appropriate	reside
appeal	credible	theory
appear	prey	variable
	region	

1. My teacher explained her _____ that if we study with a partner, we'll do better on the test.

2. Slightly more than a million people _____ in Rhode Island.

3. Small children sometimes need help choosing _____ birthday gifts for their friends.

4. The coach will excuse you for missing practice only if you have a/an _____ reason for not being there.

5. People were _____ that someone had trampled the flower garden.

6. The youngest of five siblings, Zaria was _____ to her brothers' pranks.

7. This _____ of the country is known for its mild weather.

8. In our messy home, things _____ to be disorganized, but we really do have a system that lets us keep track of everything.

9. It's hard to resist the _____ of fresh strawberries with cream.

10. The price of fruits and vegetables is _____ depending on what's in season.

11. The hikers wondered what wild animals might _____ in the woods.

12. Does your school have rules about _____ dress?

Expand Word Meanings

Read the paragraph below to learn other meanings for some of the lesson words.

If scholars want to research a civilization that mysteriously disappeared, they need to raise money. They might have to appeal to a university or museum for funds. That organization would then have to examine their case and determine what present-day society would learn from their findings. One variable the committee would consider is the method of research used. All evidence about the civilization must appear naturally, undisturbed over the years by looters or other researchers. In addition, the committee would judge the quality of the findings. Research must be original because no one can appropriate someone else's scholarship.

> **!** Four lesson words are used in a different way here. Notice how *appropriate* is a verb here instead of an adjective. In this sense, it's pronounced with a long *a* in the final syllable. Can you figure out what it and the other highlighted words mean as they are used here? Refer to page 212 to confirm meanings.

Apply Other Meanings

Complete each sentence with a highlighted word from the paragraph above.

1. She tried to _____ all the opponent's best players for her team.

2. Because I was home sick for three days, I had to _____ to my English teacher for a little more time to turn in my project.

3. Suddenly, we saw our cat _____ at the window.

4. The letter *x* is used in the equation *12 + 3 = x* to represent the _____.

5. Deer often cause car crashes when they _____ on the roadway.

6. The art department will _____ to the school board for more funding.

7. The rug was going to be thrown out, so we decided to _____ it for our clubhouse.

8. Illness is a/an _____ that will affect the total number of students who will go on the field trip.

9. Libraries often _____ to their patrons for financial support.

10. The first girl on the bus tried to _____ nearby seats for her friends.

Word Associations

Use what you know about the lesson word in italics to answer each question. Circle the letter next to the phrase that best answers the question. Be prepared to explain your answers.

1. Which activity would most *appeal* to a football fan?

   a. buying a new ball

   b. avoiding football games

   c. going to a pro football game

2. Where would an owl be most likely to *reside*?

   a. in a tree trunk

   b. in a cellar

   c. in a pond

3. Which would be an *appropriate* tool to make a hole with?

   a. screwdriver

   b. drill

   c. saw

4. Which is the most *credible* explanation of light in the night sky?

   a. a UFO

   b. a rainbow

   c. lightning

5. Who might be the *prey* of a dishonest money-making scheme?

   a. a desperate person

   b. a cautious person

   c. a capable person

6. Who might be *appalled* if served steak for dinner?

   a. a hungry person

   b. a meat eater

   c. a vegetarian

7. Which of these dates is NOT *variable*?

   a. New Year's Day

   b. Thanksgiving

   c. first day of school

8. Which state is in the northeast *region* of the United States?

   a. Texas

   b. Maine

   c. California

9. Which of these is a *theory*?

   a. why dinosaurs are extinct

   b. how many students are in your school

   c. 5 − 2 = 3

10. Which would *appear* to be most the difficult to do?

    a. standing on one leg

    b. doing two push-ups

    c. performing a back flip

Check Again

Use what you know about the lesson word in italics to complete each sentence. Be sure your sentences make sense.

1. On a farm, animals *reside* in _____

2. The *region* of the world I would most like to visit is _____

3. When people in the audience *appear* to be bored, a speaker should _____

_____

4. An *appropriate* name for a collection of stories about cats might be _____

5. A *credible* reason for being late for school might be that _____

6. The birds of *prey* flew over the open field in search of _____

_____

7. Our cell phone bill is *variable* because _____

8. If you can't finish your school project in time, you can *appeal* to _____

_____

9. One *theory* that could explain why people don't get enough sleep is _____

_____

10. People were *appalled* when they learned that the winner of the road race _____

_____

Challenge Yourself

Write Your Own

Follow the directions to write sentences with the lesson words in italics. Be sure your sentences make sense both grammatically and in meaning.

1. Write a sentence with *credible* in the fourth position.

2. Write a question exactly ten words in length using the word *appear*.

3. Write about the Minoans with *theory* in the fourth position.

Word-Solving Strategies:
Prefixes

The prefix ap-: "to," "toward," "near"

You've learned about root words and prefixes, such as *re-* and *de-*, in previous lessons. Recall that prefixes are added to the beginnings of root words. Knowing the meaning of a prefix can sometimes help you understand the meaning of a word.

Four of the lesson words have the prefix *ap-*: *appear*, *appeal*, *appalled*, and *appropriate*. In Latin, the prefix *ap-* has the meaning "to," "toward," or "near." Unlike some words, these lesson words don't have recognizable English base words. In these cases, you can't use the meaning of the prefix to help you understand what the words mean. That's because all four words are derived from Latin words, and it is the Latin word that the prefix has been added to.

The English word *appalled* comes from the Latin word *pallir*, which means "to go pale." The Latin word *proprius* means "one's own," and when we add the prefix *ap-*, we get the word *appropriate*.

Examples

Take a look at these examples of English words that are derived from Latin words with the prefix *ap-*.

ap- + *prehendere* → *apprehend*

ap- + *parer* → *appear*

ap- + *pendere* → *append*

ap- + *pretium* → *appraise*

BE CAREFUL!

The prefix *ap-* actually comes from the prefix *ad-*, which means "to," "toward," or "near." The spelling of *ad-* changes to *ap-* when it is added to a root word that begins with *p*. All of the lesson words have root words that begin with *p*; therefore, they all have *ap-* as their prefix.

Practice

Write a sentence using each of these words with the *ap-* prefix. Use a dictionary if you are not sure of the meaning of a word.

1. appointment _____

_____

2. applaud _____

_____

3. approach _____

_____

4. apply _____

_____

5. approve _____

_____

6. appendix _____

_____

Practice for Tests

Fill in the bubble next to the answer that best completes the sentence or answers the question.

1. Read this sentence.

I was *appalled* when I saw that my test score was so low.

Appalled means:
- ○ **A** satisfied
- ○ **B** sad
- ○ **C** shocked
- ○ **D** confused

2. Synonyms for *reside* are:
- ○ **A** near, close
- ○ **B** oppose, resist
- ○ **C** visit, stay
- ○ **D** live, dwell

3. The opposite of *credible* is:
- ○ **A** unbelievable
- ○ **B** incapable
- ○ **C** trustworthy
- ○ **D** reasonable

4. Which of these is a *theory?*
- ○ **A** I have two older siblings.
- ○ **B** My favorite dessert is pie.
- ○ **C** Please leave a message when you hear the tone.
- ○ **D** She is a good basketball player because she is tall.

5. When something has *appeal*, it:
- ○ **A** sounds like a bell
- ○ **B** is unlike anything else
- ○ **C** is attractive to people
- ○ **D** raises a question

6. Read this sentence:

From a distance, the mountains *appear* to be covered with moss.

Appear means:
- ○ **A** position
- ○ **B** attempt
- ○ **C** grow
- ○ **D** seem

7. A word closely associated with *prey* is:
- ○ **A** request
- ○ **B** victim
- ○ **C** plead
- ○ **D** worry

8. The opposite of *variable* is:
- ○ **A** fixed
- ○ **B** changeable
- ○ **C** uneven
- ○ **D** believable

9. If a gift is *appropriate,* it is:
- ○ **A** expensive to buy
- ○ **B** something to be worn
- ○ **C** suitable for the person
- ○ **D** taken from someone else

10. If something affects an entire *region,* it affects:
- ○ **A** a large geographic area
- ○ **B** all the cities in a state
- ○ **C** the entire United States
- ○ **D** states located along a coast

▶ **Watch** a video introduction to this passage at **vocabularyforsuccess.com**.

🔊 **Listen** to this passage at **vocabularyforsuccess.com**.

The Anasazi People
<encyclopedia entry>

For more than 1,000 years, Native Americans called the Anasazi lived in the American Southwest. They populated the region now called the Four Corners, where Utah, Arizona, New Mexico, and Colorado meet. A remarkable people, the Anasazi built structures that were thought to be the most incredible feature of their society. Then, without explanation, they left. Questions still haunt us. Why did the Anasazi leave their lives and well-constructed homes, and why did they never return?

Disappearance Before they disappeared, the Anasazi people created a complex series of roads, dams, and reservoirs. They also built impressive "apartment" buildings made of mud and plaster. Later, they carved even larger complexes out of the sides of nearby cliffs. These structures were as intricate and beautiful as any cathedral. A single dwelling might contain hundreds of rooms for living and working. There were also rooms filled with apparatus, such as ceremonial bowls, used for religious rituals. These structures were so sturdy and well-built that visitors to places such as Mesa Verde National Park in Colorado can still experience them today.

Reasons It is not known exactly why the Anasazi society ultimately did disperse. For many years, scientists assumed that drought was the reason they left. Today, there is less agreement. One theory suggests that the Anasazi's efforts to ally themselves with other groups caused their numbers to dwindle, or pare down, as they moved away. Another theory suggests that assault by groups from the outside led them to the brink of extinction.

Today, we know that when the Anasazi left, they did not entirely disappear. Many moved further east and came to be called Pueblos. Others may have been absorbed into other nations, including the Hopi and the Zuni. Even though the Anasazi society did cease to exist, the beauty of this once robust culture will not be forgotten anytime soon.

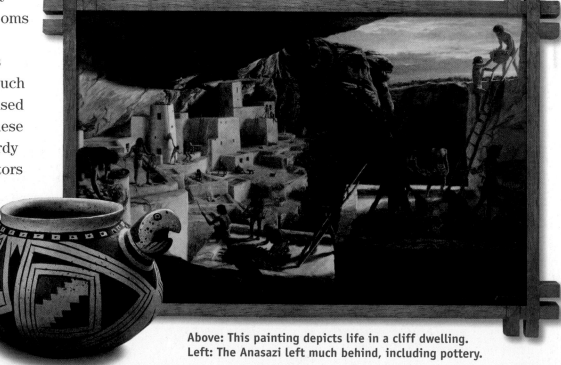

Above: This painting depicts life in a cliff dwelling.
Left: The Anasazi left much behind, including pottery.

VOCABULARY

incredible	pare
feature	assault
apparatus	brink
disperse	cease
ally	robust

TALK ABOUT IT

With a partner, answer the questions below. Use as many of the highlighted words in the selection as you can.

1. Why does it mean to be a *robust* culture? How does that desribe the Anasazi people?

2. Why do you think the Anasazi people would *ally* themselves with other groups?

Today, visitors to Cliff Palace Mesa Verde National Park in Colorado can explore these Anasazi ruins.

Word Meanings

vocabularyforsuccess.com
▶ **Watch** a video introduction for each word
◀)) **Listen** to iWords
📖 **Refer** to the online dictionary

For each highlighted word on pages 220–221, the meaning is given below. For practice with other meanings, see pages 225–227. For synonyms and antonyms, see page 240.

1. **incredible**
   (in-KRED-uh-buhl)

   (adj.) Something that is too amazing or too extraordinary to be believed is *incredible*.

2. **feature**
   (FEE-chur)

   (n.) *A feature* is an important part or characteristic of something, such as air conditioning in a car.

   (v.) When you *feature* something, you give it special importance.

3. **apparatus**
   (a-puh-RA-tuhss)

   (n.) An *apparatus* is an object or piece of equipment designed for a particular use.

   (n.) The process through which an activity is carried out is an *apparatus*, such as the *apparatus* of an organization, government, or society.

4. **disperse**
   (diss-PURSS)

   (v.) When people in a group *disperse*, they go off in different directions and the group is broken up.

5. **ally**
   v. (uh-LYE)
   n. (AL-eye)

   (v.) When you *ally* yourself with someone, you join forces and enter into a partnership.

   (n.) An *ally* is someone who helps and supports you.

6. **pare**
   (pair)

   (v.) To *pare* something down, you reduce it little by little.

7. **assault**
   (uh-SAWLT)

   (n.) An *assault* is a violent attack that does harm or intends to do harm.

   (v.) When you *assault* someone, you attack the person either physically or with words.

8. **brink**
   (breengk)

   (n.) When you are on the *brink* of something, you are just about to do it or it is just about to happen.

9. **cease**
   (seess)

   (v.) When you *cease* doing something, you stop or end what you're doing.

10. **robust**
    (roh-BUHST)

    (adj.) Someone or something that is strong, vigorous, or hearty is *robust*.

Word Talk

Each lesson word is listed here. With a partner, take turns drawing a picture to illustrate the meaning of six of the words. As one partner draws, the other partner identifies the vocabulary word.

- ally (v.)
- apparatus
- assault (n.)
- brink
- cease
- disperse
- feature (n.)
- incredible
- pare
- robust

robust

Check for Understanding

Choose the lesson word that completes each sentence. Write the word on the line provided. Some words will be used twice.

ally	brink	incredible
apparatus	cease	pare
assault	disperse	robust
	feature	

1. She worked hard to _____ her report down to the 500-word limit.

2. The librarian asked everyone to _____ talking in the reading room.

3. A well-known _____ of our town is the clock tower.

4. A projector and a laser pointer are part of the _____ we use to make presentations.

5. The crowd will _____ as soon as the game is over.

6. Most people prefer to _____ themselves with a partner who works hard.

7. I was on the _____ of solving this math problem when you interrupted me.

8. Sometimes the characters in science fiction are believable even though the stories are totally _____.

9. The _____ on the buffalo in the late nineteenth century almost made them extinct.

10. The _____ hikers had no problem completing the five-mile walk through the woods.

11. He wanted everyone to _____ playing music, as he was studying.

12. When the bus stops at our corner, ten kids _____ to their homes.

Expand Word Meanings

Read the paragraph below to learn other meanings for some of the lesson words.

The most successful societies have a strong sense of order. Each of these societies has an apparatus that can help keep things running smoothly, such as a security force. People come together in order to work toward a common goal. Staying safe is one of the most important goals of any society. Problems can occur, however, if another group tries to assault the people within a group. Those who are attacked may seek an ally nearby in order to defend themselves against these unwanted invaders. In times of trouble, a strong leader comes up with a solution that will feature an idea to bring the conflict to a peaceful end.

> Notice that some of the lesson words are used in different ways here. Look at *feature*. Here it's used as a verb to mean "have as an important part." Look at the other highlighted words. Can you figure out their meanings as they are used here? Refer to page 222 to confirm their meanings.

Apply Other Meanings

Complete each sentence with a highlighted word from the paragraph above.

1. That author writes mystery books that _____ a woman detective.

2. The government _____ made it easy for its citizens to pass new laws.

3. My next-door neighbor is my best friend and my _____ in everything.

4. Some people can _____ others with words that hurt as much as physical blows.

5. You're going to need a strong _____ or two to help you defend that unpopular idea.

6. I love movies that _____ my favorite actors.

7. The new club needed some _____ in place that would allow members to vote on others' ideas.

8. Strong winds can _____ you on a bitterly cold winter day.

9. My little brother often becomes my _____ when we both want something from Mom and Dad.

10. Teenagers usually prefer reading stories that _____ characters their own age or slightly older.

Word Associations

Use what you know about the lesson word in italics to answer each question. Circle the letter next to the phrase that best answers the question. Be prepared to explain your answers.

1. When should you *cease* exercising?
   a. when you begin to feel sick
   b. when you have been sitting for a long time
   c. when you want to challenge yourself physically

2. What is a *feature* of big-city skylines?
   a. tall trees
   b. rolling hills
   c. skyscrapers

3. Which *apparatus* might a home builder need?
   a. a saw
   b. wood
   c. blueprints

4. Which is NOT a way to *pare* an assignment down?
   a. do a little at a time
   b. do it all at once
   c. get others to help

5. When does a crowd of fans *disperse*?
   a. when a player scores a goal
   b. when the game begins
   c. when the game is over

6. Which does NOT make a person *robust*?
   a. exercise
   b. enough sleep
   c. overeating

7. Which would be a verbal *assault*?
   a. name-calling
   b. praise
   c. talking too loudly

8. Which kind of book deals most with *incredible* events?
   a. biography
   b. realistic fiction
   c. fantasy

9. Which situation would be considered to be on the *brink* of success?
   a. entering a competition
   b. being in the tournament finals
   c. finishing a ten-mile hike

10. With whom would you want to *ally* yourself to form a band?
    a. someone who sings well
    b. a fan of a famous musician
    c. people younger than you

Check Again

Use what you know about the lesson word in italics to complete each sentence. Be sure your sentences make sense.

1. If you *ally* yourself with someone, you _____

2. Seeing a unicorn in the woods would be *incredible* because _____
   _____

3. The best *feature* of our school is _____

4. When the subway doors open, passengers *disperse* because _____
   _____

5. I was on the *brink* of making a terrible mistake, but _____

6. I had to *pare* down my science report because _____

7. If you would *cease* what you are doing for five minutes, _____
   _____

8. My father always buys the most up-to-date home theater *apparatus* even though _____
   _____

9. People look *robust* when they _____

10. The victims of the hurricane suffered an *assault* _____
    _____

Challenge Yourself

Follow the directions to write sentences with the lesson words in italics. Be sure your sentences make sense both grammatically and in meaning.

1. Write a sentence with *brink* in the fifth position.

2. Write a question exactly ten words in length using the word *incredible*.

3. Write a sentence about the Southwest using the word *feature*.

Word-Solving Strategies: Context Clues

Examples

Sometimes an author will help you understand the meaning of a word by giving an example. Reread this sentence from "The Anasazi People."

There were also rooms filled with apparatus, such as ceremonial bowls, used for religious rituals.

Note that the word **apparatus** is followed by "ceremonial bowls," as an example of an item "used for religious rituals." The words *like* or *such as* often signal that an example follows.

BE CAREFUL!

The words *like* and *such as* don't always signal an example. Read this sentence:

Apparatus such as these have been found in other ancient pueblo communities.

In this sentence, the words *such as* make a comparison.

Examples can also be set off by dashes or commas, so also watch for punctuation clues.

Practice

A. Write the highlighted word and its meaning in the first two boxes. In the third box, write the example that helped you get the meaning.

We have been puzzled by conundrums similar to the mysterious disappearance of the Anasazi. In 1587, Englishmen led by John White established a colony on Roanoke Island. Soon after they arrived, White returned to England for provisions—grain, seeds, and other things needed for survival. White expected to be back in three months, but it took three years. When he returned, everyone had vanished. One conjecture that researchers offer is that the colonists went to live with a native tribe.

WORD	MEANING	EXAMPLE

B. Write a sentence for each of the highlighted words from the paragraph above. Be sure to use an example as a context clue.

1. _____

2. _____

3. _____

Practice for Tests

Fill in the bubble next to the answer that best completes the sentence or answers the question.

1. Read the sentence.

   The blizzard was an *assault* on the midwestern states.

   Assault means:

   ○ **A** winter season
   ○ **B** seasonal change
   ○ **C** violent attack
   ○ **D** large increase

2. The opposite of *disperse* is:
   ○ **A** scatter
   ○ **B** dispel
   ○ **C** distribute
   ○ **D** gather

3. A person on the *brink* is:
   ○ **A** not thinking about anything
   ○ **B** walking on the edge of a road
   ○ **C** regretting doing something
   ○ **D** about to do something

4. You *pare* something down when you:
   ○ **A** make it smaller
   ○ **B** chop it in half
   ○ **C** cut off the ends
   ○ **D** slice it up

5. If something is *incredible,* it is:
   ○ **A** too ordinary to be interesting
   ○ **B** very frightening
   ○ **C** too amazing to believe
   ○ **D** too terrible to think about

6. Read this sentence:

   Adobe pueblos were a *feature* of Anasazi communities.

   Feature means:

   ○ **A** method of construction
   ○ **B** type of housing
   ○ **C** surviving remains
   ○ **D** important characteristic

7. A word closely associated with *apparatus* is:
   ○ **A** window
   ○ **B** equipment
   ○ **C** opening
   ○ **D** visibility

8. Whom would you *ally* with?
   ○ **A** a stranger
   ○ **B** a competitor
   ○ **C** a partner
   ○ **D** an enemy

9. The music will *cease* when:
   ○ **A** the conductor comes out
   ○ **B** the audience gets bored
   ○ **C** the concert is over
   ○ **D** everyone finds a seat

10. A *robust* person is:
    ○ **A** very overweight
    ○ **B** strong and healthy
    ○ **C** weak and sickly
    ○ **D** fragile

▶ **Watch** a video introduction to this passage at **vocabularyforsuccess.com**.

🔊 **Listen** to this passage at **vocabularyforsuccess.com**.

The Easter Island Puzzle

<interview>

Interviewer: Welcome, Dr. Sanchez. You've spent many years studying the history of a tiny island with a mysterious past. Tell us more.

Dr. Luisa Sanchez: Yes, Easter Island is certainly tiny. It's just 64 square miles—the size of Washington, D.C. Today it's part of Chile and about 2,000 people live there, but long ago, an ancient, mysterious culture existed on the island. They built truly astonishing statues and left behind writings impossible to decode.

Interviewer: Tell me about those statues.

Dr. Luisa Sanchez: There are nearly 900 of these incredible statues, most of which are now lying on their sides. They must have been very dramatic, as some stand 40 feet high and weigh 80 tons! We believe that people created them to honor their ancestors, perhaps including them in some kind of ritual.

Clearly, making the statues was hard work, not some leisure activity. We know the statues were carved from volcanic stone on one part of the island, then moved elsewhere. We believe these people used sled-like log structures to transport the statues. They must have cut down many trees for that purpose. We've tried to duplicate the process of moving the statues ourselves. It was very difficult! We may never know the ancients' motive for moving them. But we do know that by 1722, when the Dutch explorer Jacob Roggeveen arrived, there were few people left, little food, and no trees.

Interviewer: I suppose this bald island and its huge statues must have been a bizarre sight!

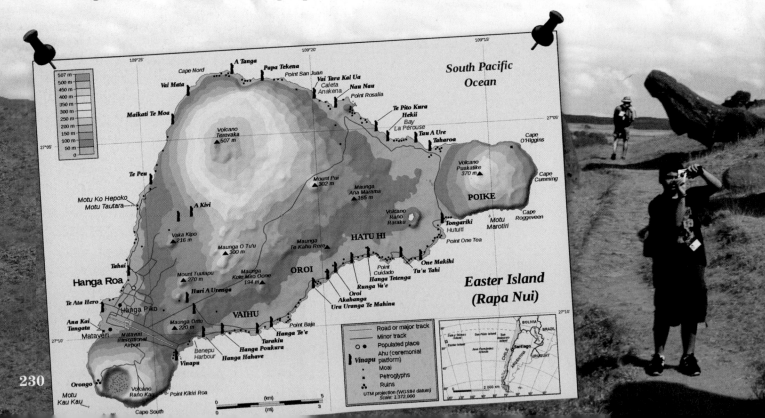

decode motive
dramatic bizarre
ritual premise
leisure implicate
duplicate reference

Dr. Luisa Sanchez: It was. One premise among scientists is that the ancients cut down all their trees in order to move their statues. They didn't even leave enough wood to make fishing boats. Other experts implicate rats in this mystery. Their theory makes reference to animal habits. Rats, they say, would have thrived on a deserted island. They would have eaten any remaining seeds that could have been used to grow crops. Unfortunately, we'll never know for certain.

Interviewer: Amazing! Thank you for taking the time to discuss the mysteries of Easter Island.

Far left: This map shows the location of statues on Easter Island.

Near left: This visitor stands amidst the statues.

TALK ABOUT IT

With a partner, answer the questions below. Use as many of the highlighted words in the selection as you can.

1. Why did scientists *implicate* rats? What kinds of things might the rats have eaten and what was the result?

2. Do you think that someday scientists might be able to *decode* the mystery of Easter Island? Why or why not?

Word Meanings

For each highlighted word on pages 230–231, the meaning is given below. For practice with other meanings, see pages 235–237. For synonyms and antonyms, see page 240.

vocabularyforsuccess.com

▶ **Watch** a video introduction for each word

◀)) **Listen** to iWords

📖 **Refer** to the online dictionary

1. decode
(dee-KODE)

(v.) When you *decode* something, you change it from an unreadable message of letters, numbers, or symbols into language that can be understood. You figure it out.

2. dramatic
(druh-MA-tik)

(adj.) Something that is *dramatic* is very noticeable or striking in appearance or manner.

(adj.) Something is *dramatic* when it relates to the theater and to acting.

3. ritual
(RICH-oo-uhl)

(n.) A *ritual* is a set of actions always performed in the same way as part of a ceremony or custom.

4. leisure
(LEE-zhur)

(adj.) A *leisure* activity is a hobby or something you do during the time you are free from work or other responsibilities.

5. duplicate
v. (DOO-pluh-kayt)
n. (DOO-pluh-kit)

(v.) When you *duplicate* the actions of another, you try to do something exactly as it was done before.

(n.) A *duplicate* is an exact copy.

6. motive
(MOH-tiv)

(n.) A *motive* is the need or desire that makes a person do something.

7. bizarre
(bi-ZAHR)

(adj.) Something that is *bizarre* is extremely unusual or out of the ordinary.

8. premise
(PREM-iss)

(n.) A *premise* is a statement or conclusion that is accepted as true.

9. implicate
(IM-pluh-kayt)

(v.) When you *implicate,* you say, imply, or hint at something. You might *implicate* someone by saying he or she is connected to an action or event, such as when you reveal the name of the person you saw eating the last piece of pie.

10. reference
(REF-renss)

(n.) If you make a *reference,* you mention or refer to some fact or idea.

(adj.) A *reference* source is a book, publication, or document that has information you use when writing about a topic.

Word Talk

Each lesson word has been placed in a category. With a partner, discuss and list items that belong in each category. Compare your results with those of another pair of students.

Familiar *Rituals*	*Leisure* Activities

Things You Might *Decode*	Things You Can *Duplicate*	*Motives* for Working Hard	Concepts That Are *Bizarre*

Things That Could *Implicate* You	A *Premise* About Parents	Actions That Are *Dramatic*	A *Reference* You Might Make on the First Day of School

Check for Understanding

Choose the lesson word that completes each sentence. Write the word on the line provided. Some words will be used twice.

bizarre	duplicate	premise
decode	implicate	reference
dramatic	leisure	ritual
	motive	

1. In his book report, the student made a/an _____ to the author's love of dogs.

2. Eating pancakes for breakfast on Sunday morning is a/an _____ in our house.

3. Rebecca was able to _____ the message by figuring out which letter each number corresponded to.

4. More than six feet tall and with curly red hair, our English teacher is a very _____ figure.

5. There are few weather events as _____ as a snowstorm in summer.

6. Our teacher believes in the _____ that every student can do well.

7. If you _____ what I did, your results should be the same.

8. The rug is dirty, and the paw prints _____ the dog.

9. No one seems to have much _____ time anymore.

10. They tried to understand the child's _____ for throwing a tantrum.

11. Although it was the best salad we had ever made, somehow we could never _____ another one that tasted as good.

12. Families often make a/an _____ of their holiday celebrations.

Expand Word Meanings

Read the paragraph below to learn other meanings for some of the lesson words.

My friend Noah has written a story about Jacob Roggeveen, the Dutch explorer who was the first European to visit Easter Island. Noah used an encyclopedia as his major reference source for the facts about Roggeveen. Noah learned that Roggeveen called this land Easter Island because he arrived there on Easter in 1722. Noah also used his imagination when he wrote. His story has lots of dialogue, with Roggeveen and his crew talking and reacting to what they see. Our class is doing a dramatic reading of Noah's story. I'm helping to organize it. I promised to make a duplicate of the text for each actor.

> **!** Some of the lesson words are used in different ways here. Look at *reference*. Here it means the book or source you use to get your facts. Look at the other highlighted words. Can you figure out the meanings of the words as they are used here? Refer to page 232 to confirm the meanings.

Apply Other Meanings

Complete each sentence with a highlighted word from the paragraph above.

1. At the end of our report we are supposed to list each _____ source we used.

2. My grandmother told me that before there were copy machines, people had to use carbon paper to make a _____.

3. Many of the kids who are interested in acting want to start a _____ society at our school.

4. What would it be like to have an exact _____ of an Easter Island statue in your backyard?

5. Rhiannon didn't need to use a _____ book to write her story because it was fiction.

6. I was so happy when the theater company asked to do a _____ adaptation of my short story.

7. Some people say that everyone has a double, but I don't believe there's a _____ of me anywhere.

8. If you can't get the library to use a _____ text, look for an Internet version.

9. At the café's open mike night, Nicole delivered a _____ monologue.

10. This poster is a _____ of a famous painting that hangs in a museum.

Word Associations

Use what you know about the lesson word in italics to answer each question. Circle the letter next to the phrase that best answers the question. Be prepared to explain your answers.

1. Which profession might require you to *decode*?

   a. nutritionist
   b. textbook writer
   c. spy

2. If your *premise* is that skiing is fun, you would think:

   a. everyone should try it
   b. nobody should try it
   c. people should promise to try it

3. Which activity might someone do in their *leisure* time?

   a. work in an office
   b. work in the garden
   c. drive to work

4. Which is the most likely place for a *ritual*?

   a. grocery store
   b. public library
   c. temple

5. If you make a *reference* to your mother, which is most likely true?

   a. you assist her
   b. you mention her
   c. you ignore her

6. Which animal would many people consider most *bizarre*?

   a. a purple mouse
   b. an angry dog
   c. an unfriendly cat

7. Which would be the most *dramatic* gesture?

   a. writing a note to an actor
   b. making a phone call to a friend
   c. giving someone a dozen roses

8. Which action might you want to *duplicate*?

   a. falling off your bike
   b. scoring a goal
   c. losing a library book

9. What might *implicate* you in a prank?

   a. being one of the victims
   b. visiting someone out of town
   c. pointing and laughing

10. What is NOT a *motive* for doing chores?

    a. getting your room organized
    b. earning some money
    c. finishing your homework

Check Again

Use what you know about the lesson word in italics to complete each sentence. Be sure your sentences make sense.

1. The most *bizarre* thing I ever saw was _____

2. In my *leisure* time, I like to _____

3. It would be hard to *decode* a message that was _____

4. It is overly *dramatic* to _____

5. The difference between *ritual* and habit is _____
_____

6. My *motive* for working hard at school is _____

7. A possible *premise* for an article about middle schoolers is _____
_____

8. In her speech to the whole school, the principal made *reference* to _____
_____

9. I didn't want to *implicate* a friend, but _____
_____

10. I wanted to *duplicate* his amazing dive, but _____
_____

Challenge Yourself

Follow the directions to write sentences with the lesson words in italics. Be sure your sentences make sense both grammatically and in meaning.

1. Write a sentence with the word *dramatic* in the fifth position.

2. Write a sentence exactly nine words in length using *duplicate* as a noun.

3. Write a sentence about Easter Island, using the word *bizarre* in your sentence.

Word-Solving Strategies:
Context Clues

Antonyms

Sometimes an author helps you understand an unfamiliar word by giving you clues that mean the opposite. Reread this sentence from "The Easter Island Puzzle."

> Clearly, making the statues was hard work, not some leisure activity.

The opposite of **leisure** is *work*. The antonym helps you figure out the meaning of **leisure**. If you cannot figure out the meaning of a word from its antonym, you can look the word up in an Internet dictionary. This resource will help clarify usage.

BE CAREFUL!

The words *no* and *not* often signal an antonym, but not always. Read this sentence:

> *People were amazed—no, they were awestruck—by the statues.*

Here the word *no* does not signal an antonym. *Amazed* and *awestruck* are related in meaning, but *awestruck* is stronger.

Practice

A. Write the highlighted word and its antonym in the first two boxes. Then write the meaning of the highlighted word.

> The Netherlands seems so peaceable today that it's hard to imagine how **aggressive** the Dutch once were about exploring the world. Far from being laid-back, Dutch explorers were **intrepid**. When Jacob Roggeveen came upon Easter Island, he was looking for the "Southern Continent" of Australia. Ice and rough weather made him abandon the idea. He seems halfhearted compared with Henry Hudson, who was **obsessed** with finding the Northwest Passage. Hudson never gave up and literally died trying.

WORD	ANTONYM	WORD MEANING

B. Write a sentence for each of the highlighted words from the paragraph above. Use an antonym as a context clue.

1. _____

2. _____

3. _____

Practice for Tests

Fill in the bubble next to the answer that best completes the sentence or answers the question.

1. Read this sentence.

   Who had a *motive* for wanting our team to lose the game?

   Motive means:
   - **A** plot
   - **B** scheme
   - **C** desire
   - **D** enemy

2. When you *decode* something, you:
   - **A** hide its meaning
   - **B** put it in writing
   - **C** proofread it
   - **D** reveal its meaning

3. A synonym for *bizarre* is:
   - **A** odd
   - **B** imaginary
   - **C** indifferent
   - **D** exciting

4. When you *duplicate* a letter, you:
   - **A** post it online
   - **B** edit and publish it
   - **C** print it out
   - **D** copy it exactly

5. An example of a *leisure* activity is:
   - **A** taking a shower
   - **B** washing the dishes
   - **C** going to the movies
   - **D** mowing the lawn

6. Read this sentence.

   Her letter made *reference* to something that happened long ago.

   Reference means:
   - **A** mocking fun
   - **B** history
   - **C** respect
   - **D** mention

7. A statement is a *premise* if it is:
   - **A** proved to be true
   - **B** accepted as true
   - **C** based on false data
   - **D** a complete fantasy

8. If you *implicate* someone in an act, you:
   - **A** imply that she was involved
   - **B** clear her of any blame
   - **C** invite her to be a part
   - **D** ignore her actions

9. A *dramatic* gesture is:
   - **A** insincere
   - **B** hardly noticed
   - **C** extreme
   - **D** quiet

10. A *ritual* is performed:
    - **A** haphazardly
    - **B** the same way every time
    - **C** in time to music
    - **D** without thinking about it

Synonyms and Antonyms

In the following Word Bank, you will find synonyms and antonyms for some of the words in Lessons 19–21. (Remember: Some words have both synonyms and antonyms.) Study these words; then complete the exercises below.

machine	edge	dull	unbelievable	middle	immediate
attacker	copy	limit	dwell	reasonable	disgusted

A. For each sentence, fill in the blank with a SYNONYM for the word in boldface.

1. Claire explained to the science fair judges that her invention was a clever

_____ hidden inside a complicated **apparatus**.

2. The movie took its viewers to the **brink** of terror and then to the cutting

_____ of comedy.

3. In order to **duplicate** the painting, the artist had to _____ the colors and style used in the original.

4. The audience was **appalled** by the play's ending and left the theater with

_____ looks on their faces.

5. The squirrels _____ in the tree next to the hole in which the chipmunks **reside**.

B. For each sentence, fill in the blank with an ANTONYM for the word in boldface.

6. Hector's letter had many _____ requests, but it also contained one **bizarre** demand that most people felt was not acceptable.

7. After the thieves searched for **prey** to rob, one of their victims was able to identify the

tallest _____ as the person who threatened him.

8. The canoe drifted from the _____ of the river to the **brink** of the waterfall.

9. The **dramatic** way she expressed herself was preferable to his _____ rambling monotone.

10. The police were looking for **credible** evidence, but all they heard were _____ tall tales.

Word Study: Denotation and Connotation

Every word has a denotation, or literal meaning that you would find in a dictionary. Some words also have connotations, which are positive or negative feelings that these words bring to mind. Some words are neutral, which means they are neither positive nor negative in connotation. Here are some examples.

POSITIVE	NEGATIVE	NEUTRAL
cheerful	manic	pleased
home	hovel	house

Some words have similar denotations but different connotations. For example:

POSITIVE	NEGATIVE	NEUTRAL
skipped	stomped	hopped

Knowing the connotation of words can help writvary their writing and help readers understand the writer's intent. For example:

We hopped on the grass. We stomped on the grass. We skipped on the grass.

Practice

A. Circle the word in parentheses that has the connotation (positive, negative, or neutral) given at the beginning of the sentence.

neutral **1.** The club president (**requested**, **ordered**) the members to sit down.

positive **2.** The guest made a (**graceful**, **appropriate**) bow to the host.

negative **3.** Following the gas explosion, lava will (**appear**, **erupt**) from the volcano.

positive **4.** He looked for an (**acquaintance**, **ally**) in the crowd.

neutral **5.** The statue of the horse was (**large**, **enormous**).

positive **6.** The view of the pyramids from the airplane was (**breathtaking**, **interesting**)

negative **7.** We were (**upset**, **appalled**) when we saw the mess in the kitchen.

B. Work with a partner. Write a plus sign (+) if the word has a positive connotation; write a minus sign (–) if the word has a negative connotation. Put a zero (0) if the word is neutral.

1. feature ☐   3. weak ☐   5. assault ☐   7. robust ☐

2. honor ☐   4. reside ☐   6. incredible ☐   8. disperse ☐

Vocabulary for Comprehension

Read the following passage, in which some of the words you have studied in Lessons 19–21 appear in boldface type. Then answer questions 1–6.

What Happened to the Clovis People?

North America has a civilization that disappeared mysteriously. The people are called the Clovis, and they lived in every **region** of North America about 13,000 years ago. They
5 were once thought to be the first humans here, but that **theory** has been challenged, causing scholars to **cease** assigning them the title "first Americans." Although they may not have been the first humans to **reside** here, Clovis was
10 America's first **robust**, well-established culture.

The Clovis people were primarily big game hunters. They hunted large-bodied animals that are now extinct. A characteristic **feature** of Clovis culture is the unique fluted stone spear
15 point they used in hunting. Their **motive** for becoming big game hunters instead of hunter-gatherer-fishers was survival. Clues **implicate** drought as a possible reason for their big game targets. Fish might have been scarce.

20 Clovis civilization survived for about 500 years. It is not certain what happened, but their end was abrupt. They disappeared at the same time that the large animals they hunted did. The Clovis may have hunted the big game to
25 extinction and then fallen **prey** to extinction themselves. Another explanation is more **dramatic**. A natural disaster may have killed off the big game as well as the Clovis people.

1. In line 3, **region** means
   - A mountain range
   - B plains area
   - C river valley
   - D geographic area

2. Another word for **reside** (line 9) is
   - A leave
   - B live
   - C visit
   - D develop

3. A **feature** (line 13) of an ancient civilization is
   - A an important characteristic
   - B a discovered artifact
   - C a primitive tool
   - D a possible explanation

4. When you have a **motive** (line 15), you have
   - A a hunger
   - B a method
   - C a need
   - D a rule

5. When you **implicate** (line 17) something, you
   - A blame
   - B make it better
   - C explain a problem
   - D prove a theory

6. In line 25, **prey** means
   - A hunter
   - B to hunt
   - C victim
   - D a purpose

Using Context

Circle the word that best completes each sentence. Note that the choices are related forms of the vocabulary words in the box.

abundant	decline	impose
appeal	degenerate	incredible
appear	formal	normal
appropriate	foster	photosynthesis
concept	infection	recreation
consequence	implicate	reside

1. Our town's new **(recreational/residential)** facility includes an indoor basketball court that the community leagues can use.

2. The students were praised for behaving **(appropriately/abundantly)** by following the rules during their trip to the museum.

3. We hope it won't be an **(implication/imposition)** if we stay with you for a few days more than we had planned.

4. Juliano **(infected/fostered)** me with his cold, so now I am sick, too.

5. My cousin will be **(appealing/appearing)** onstage this Friday at the local theater.

6. The plan for the new park is only **(consequential/conceptual)** right now and won't be finalized for at least three months.

7. The **(formality/abundance)** of the dinner required the boys who were attending to wear jackets and ties.

8. He has a/an **(degenerative/infective)** illness that will cause the weakness in his legs to get worse over time.

9. We **(normally/incredibly)** take a walk after dinner, but our plan was interrupted by the storm.

10. The health of that tree is **(photosynthesizing/declining)** because of the extreme drought, and I'm worried it might die.

Analogies

Read each sentence stem carefully. Then complete the sentence so that it makes sense. Use the relationship between the words in italics to help you.

1. A good *critique* helps a writer understand what he or she did well in addition to which areas need improvement, while a review that makes *reference* only to what the writer could do better isn't as helpful because _____

_____

2. A *theory* is a guess based on facts, while a *doctrine* is _____

_____

3. A *robust* government is strong and doing well, while a government that has experienced a *downfall* is _____

_____

4. The temperature outside of my house is *variable* because it changes with the seasons, while the temperature inside my house is *uniform* because _____

_____

5. A small animal that is by itself might easily fall *prey* to a larger animal that is hunting it, while an animal that is able to *ally* itself with a group is better protected because

_____

_____

6. The *norms* for greeting another person in the United States include shaking hands and asking, "How are you?" while the *ritual* in another country might include _____

_____

7. An example of a *benefit* to moving to a new neighborhood may be safer streets, while an example of a negative *impact* of moving to a new neighborhood may be _____

_____

8. You should buy only the amount of fresh food you can eat in a short period because it will spoil, but you can buy *durable* items in *bulk* because _____

_____

Word Relationships

Read each question carefully. Think about the relationship between the two vocabulary words in italics. Then write an explanation that answers each question.

1. Why might we want to *seek* different forms of *energy* to run our cars?

_____

_____

_____

2. Why is it important to know which *species* live in an *ecosystem*?

_____

_____

_____

3. What outdoor *leisure* activity might *enrich* a person's life? Explain your answer.

_____

_____

_____

4. Why does a police detective try to *decode* the information contained in the *random* clues left at a crime scene?

_____

_____

_____

5. What is one reason an *authority* figure might want to appear *credible*?

_____

_____

_____

6. What might be a *motive* for one country to *invade* a neighboring country?

_____

_____

_____

Generating Sentences

Follow the directions to write sentences with the vocabulary words in italics. Be sure your sentences make sense both grammatically and in meaning.

1. Use the word *dramatic* in a sentence.

_____

_____

2. Use the word *parasite* in a sentence that is at least 8 words long.

_____

_____

3. Use the word *abnormal* in the second position in a sentence that is exactly 13 words.

_____

_____

4. Use the word *disperse* in a sentence of 14 words to describe nature.

_____

_____

5. Use the word *architecture* in the fourth position of a question.

_____

_____

Extend Your Sentence

Choose one of your sentences and turn it into a paragraph. Use at least four other words from Units 5–7 in your paragraph.

_____

_____

_____

_____

_____

_____

246

Index

A
abnormal, 188
abundant, 198
accurate, 106
achievable, 72
adequate, 126
advance, 126
aerial, 82
airborne, 58
ally, 222
alter, 72
anticipated, 126
appalled, 212
apparatus, 222
appeal, 212
appear, 212
approach, 4
appropriate, 212
architecture, 188
area, 38
argument, 14
assault, 222
assess, 3
assist, 24
atlas, 58
atmosphere, 82
authority, 198

Antonyms, 32, 66, 100, 134, 172, 206, 240

B
barren, 38
barrier, 92
benefit, 144
bias, 4
bizarre, 232
brink, 222
bulk, 178
buoy, 92

C
category, 154
cease, 222
challenge, 82
chronology, 14
circumstance, 126
civilization, 116
claim, 48
classic, 188
climate, 82
collide, 72
columns, 188
commenced, 178
compatible, 126

compile, 106
concept, 198
confer, 14
consequence, 154
constellation, 116
construct, 4
consume, 154
contact, 106
control, 24
copious, 164
cornerstone, 198
correspond, 106
counsel, 116
credible, 212
critique, 164
crust, 72
cultivate, 24
culture, 116
cycle, 82

Context Clues
Antonyms, 150, 238
Contrast/Antonyms, 88
Definitions/Explanation, 112
Embedded Definitions, 30
Examples, 64, 228
Inferences, 184
Inference/Misdirected Clues, 160
Punctuation, 10
Restatement/Synonyms, 44
Synonyms, 204

D
debate, 14
debris, 92
decline, 164
decode, 232
decompose, 154
deed, 116
degenerate, 164
deluge, 92
deplete, 164
despite, 82
detect, 164
devoted, 106
dignity, 188
disperse, 222
distribute, 4
doctrine, 198
document, 14
dominance, 126
downfall, 198
dramatic, 232
duplicate, 232
durable, 188

E
ecosystem, 144
embark, 48
enable, 58
encounter, 106
energy, 144
enormous, 188
enrich, 178
entrust, 48
erosion, 92
estimate, 106
evident, 24
expand, 82
explanation, 4

F
factor, 144
feat, 38
feature, 222
formal, 178
foster, 164
foundation, 126
fraught, 38
fulfill, 24
fungus, 154

G
global, 58

H
haphazard, 4
hardship, 82
hemisphere, 58
host, 154
hypothesis, 4

I
identical, 106
impact, 154
implicate, 232
impose, 198
inaccessible, 92
incapable, 92
incredible, 222
infection, 154
inferences, 178
ingenuity, 24
initial, 38
intern, 24
interpret, 4

invade, 164
invaluable, 24
invariable, 72
issue, 4

L
landscape, 72
latent, 24
legacy, 24
leisure, 232
likewise, 144

M
mantle, 72
mass, 92
maximum, 144
migrate, 38
minimal, 106
mobile, 24
mosaic, 188
motive, 232

Multiple Meaning Words, 7,
   17, 27, 41, 51, 61, 75, 85, 95,
   109, 119, 129, 147, 157, 167,
   181, 191, 201, 215, 225, 235

N
nevertheless, 178
normal, 188
norms, 188
nuisance, 126

O
obtainable, 72
ordeal, 82
orient, 116
origin, 58

P
parasite, 154
pare, 222

photosynthesis, 144
plague, 126
plenty, 198
population, 116
portion, 106
premier, 198
premise, 232
prey, 212
prone, 144
prospect, 48
prow, 38

R
random, 178
range, 198
ransack, 48
reassess, 14
reconstruct, 14
recreation, 144
recycling, 164
redistribute, 14
reference, 232
region, 212
regulation, 116
reinterpret, 14
report, 178
research, 14
reside, 212
restrict, 58
risk, 92
ritual, 232
robust, 222

S
scribe, 178
seek, 154
signal, 72
source, 82
species, 164
stern, 38
superlative, 116

Synonyms, 32, 66, 100,
   134, 172, 206, 240

T
theory, 212
trade, 126
transition, 48
translate, 48
transmit, 48
transport, 48
trek, 48

U
undertake, 48
uniform, 178

V
variable, 212
vessel, 92
vicinity, 38

W
widespread, 38
witness, 58

Word Parts
   Prefixes, 20, 170, 218
   Roots, 54, 122, 194
   Suffixes, 78, 132

Word Study
   Denotation and Connotation,
      33, 135, 241
   Idioms, 67, 173
   Proverbs, 101, 207